ROUTLEDGE LIBRARY EDITIONS: EDUCATION

EDUCATIONAL THEORY AND ITS FOUNDATION DISCIPLINES

EDUCATIONAL THEORY AND ITS FOUNDATION DISCIPLINES

Edited by
PAUL H. HIRST

Volume 142

 Routledge
Taylor & Francis Group

LONDON AND NEW YORK

First published in 1983

This edition first published in 2012
by Routledge
2 Park Square, Milton Park, Abingdon, Oxfordshire OX14 4RN

Simultaneously published in the USA and Canada
by Routledge
711 Third Avenue, New York, NY 10017

First issued in paperback 2014

Routledge is an imprint of the Taylor and Francis Group, an informa company

British Library Cataloguing in Publication Data
A catalogue record for this book is available from the British Library

ISBN 13: 978-0-415-68944-1 (Volume 142)
ISBN 13: 978-0-415-75089-9 (pbk)

Publisher's Note
The publisher has gone to great lengths to ensure the quality of this reprint but points out that some imperfections in the original copies may be apparent.

Disclaimer
The publisher has made every effort to trace copyright holders and would welcome correspondence from those they have been unable to trace.

Educational theory and its foundation disciplines

Edited by

Paul H. Hirst

Routledge & Kegan Paul

London and New York

First published in 1983
Reprinted 1987
by Routledge & Kegan Paul Ltd
11 New Fetter Lane, London EC4P 4EE

Published in the USA by
Routledge and Kegan Paul Inc.
in association with Methuen Inc.
29 West 35th Street, New York NY 10001

Set in IBM Press Roman, 11 on 13pt
and printed in Great Britain by
T. J. Press (Padstow) Ltd, Padstow, Cornwall

Library of Congress Cataloging in Publication Data

Educational theory and its foundation disciplines.

Includes bibliographical references.
1. Education – Addresses, essays, lectures. 2. Education –
Philosophy – Addresses, essays, lectures.
I. Hirst, Paul Heywood.
LB41.E3417   1983   370'.1   83-11157

ISBN 0–7100–9763–8

Contents

Contents

Brian Davies
Professor of Education
University of London
Chelsea College

Introduction

The publication in 1966 of a collection of papers under the title *The Study of Education*, edited by Professor J.W. Tibble,[1] inaugurated a new era in the character of educational studies in many British colleges and universities. In that volume it was argued hard that educational theory is necessarily dependent on the development of a series of contributory disciplines with recognised academic roots quite outside educational studies and a number of distinguished professors sought to map the current contributions of particular disciplines. They covered not only recent achievements in the well-established areas of educational psychology and the history of education but also the exciting work then being developed by quite new techniques in both philosophy of education and sociology of education. At this time many courses for both intending and experienced teachers came to have a sharply differentiated structure with major elements devoted explicitly to the separate disciplines. A large series of books in 'The Students Library of Education' under the editorship of the contributors to Professor Tibble's volume did much to promote the study of education in these terms.[2]

Since that period the nature of educational theory, its relationship to educational practice and the significance of the disciplines for it have been the subject of important critical discussions. Each of the distinct disciplines considered

1

in the 1966 collection has also undergone major shifts in content and methods. This present volume has therefore been designed simply to take a look at how things now stand in these particular matters. New organisations for educational studies have, of course, emerged and their appropriateness for many purposes is not in dispute. They are, however, not the direct concern of these papers. The nature of educational theory as such, rather than organisations of it for teaching purposes, and the contributions to it of what continue to be the major disciplines on which it draws remain fundamental issues. It is these that are addressed in this collection.

Four of the five papers published here had their origins in public lectures to mark the centenary of the first series of lectures given in the University of Cambridge for intending teachers. They are printed here for the first time. The fifth paper, by Professor Davies, has been largely re-written for this volume but uses material previously published elsewhere. Each author has been encouraged to express his personal point of view on developments in his particular domain. Three of the authors contributed the parallel papers in Professor Tibble's 1966 collection.

Notes

1 J.W. Tibble (ed.), *The Study of Education*, London, Routledge & Kegan Paul, 1966.
2 The Students' Library of Education, Series Founding General Editor J.W. Tibble, published Routledge and Kegan Paul.

1 Educational theory

Paul H. Hirst

In my contribution to Professor J.W. Tibble's volume *The Study of Education*[1] I sought to characterise educational theory as a domain of practical theory, concerned with formulating and justifying principles of action for a range of practical activities. Because of their concern for practical principles I sharply distinguished domains of practical theory from domains concerned simply with purely theoretical knowledge. The function of the latter is primarily explanation. The function of the former is primarily the determination of practice. The one is concerned with achieving rational understanding, the other with achieving rational action. In this approach I was in major respects at variance with that set out several years previously by Professor D.J. O'Connor in his influential book *An Introduction to the Philosophy of Education.*[2] He had argued that though the term theory could be used for 'a set or system of rules or a collection of precepts which guide or control actions of various kinds',[3] it is better used as in the natural sciences for a hypothesis or logically inter-connected set of hypotheses that have been confirmed by observation. In this sense we have 'standards by which we can assess the value and use of any claimant to the title of "theory". In particular this sense of the word will enable us to judge the value of the various (and often conflicting) theories that are put forward by writers on education.'[4]

He concluded: 'we can summarise this discussion by saying that the word "theory" as it is used in educational contexts is generally a courtesy title. It is justified only where we are applying well established experimental findings in psychology or sociology to the practice of education. And even here we should be aware that the conjectural gap between our theories and the facts on which they rest is sufficiently wide to make our logical consciences uneasy. We can hope that the future development of the social sciences will narrow this gap and this hope gives an incentive for developing these sciences.'[5] It seemed to me then, as it seems to me now, in spite of all Professor O'Connor says, critical for the development of educational practice that we hold hard to developing educational theory of a kind that is fully adequate to the nature of the educational enterprise. And to this end we should resist the seductions of a much more limited paradigm of 'theory' taken from another area, however prestigious its claims.

The differences (and agreements) between myself and Professor O'Connor were sharpened in an exchange of papers between us subsequently published in *New Essays in the Philosophy of Education*, edited by G. Langford and D.J. O'Connor.[6] We agree that all theory is concerned with explanation, but to my mind the explanation of human activities in an area like education involves not only the sciences, including the social sciences, but also matters of beliefs and values. Reasons as well as causes enter into the business, mental concepts as well as the empirical concepts of the sciences are involved. If we agree acceptable theories are to be refutable, refutation is for me not confined to the form it takes in the sciences. We agree that educational theory is concerned with 'improving' and 'guiding' practice, but for me that is more than a technical matter for a scientific form of educational theory, on the assumption that the values involved come from outside the theory itself. Of course, if I insist that the debate of educational ends as well as means comes within the theory, because to my mind the development of rational practice demands that debate and because ends and means are not ultimately separable, I must accept that the theory must incorporate all the confusions of contemporary debate about values. I must accept too that at present the logic of practical reasoning is unclear and that the structure of educational theory is therefore uncertain. But I do not despair of our progressively making our educational practice more rationally defensible, indeed I think we are slowly doing that. What is more, I see no reason to think that the logic of practical reasoning will forever elude us. After all, the elucidation of the logic of discourse can only be discerned after the emergence of acceptable paradigms of the discourse. Even in scientific discourse that logic is still a matter of dispute, whilst in the practical domain acceptable sophisticated theories are still in the making.

This second debate with Professor O'Connor has left me unrepentant in seeing educational theory as primarily the domain which seeks to develop rational principles for educational practice. To this end it draws, of course, on all the theoretical knowledge available in the social sciences. Educational psychology and sociology of education are precisely those sub-areas of psychology and sociology that are of use in this way. But it also draws on history, philosophy and much else besides; all that is significant for the formulation and justification of its rational principles. And if educational theory is a composite area of this kind, I remain unrepentant in regarding its unity as the unity of a consistent set of principles of practice at which it aims, not that of one vast theoretical integration of the contributory disciplines.

By the early 1970s, however, it was becoming clear that even if this view of the nature of educational theory is accepted, much more has to be said about the way in which the contributory disciplines are related to practical principles. Developments at that time within these disciplines only served to accentuate their radically different characters and the limited significance of any one or even all of these domains in the formulation of practical principles. Each discipline, even when concerned with educational practice,

5

clearly has its own concepts, employing these to ask its own distinctive theoretical questions, questions that are essentially, say, philosophical, psychological or historical in nature and not practical. The conclusions reached in each area, however focused on matters of educational practice, are again philosophical, psychological or historical in character and are not themselves principles for practice. The disciplines cannot tackle any given practical questions as such for each tackles questions which are peculiar to itself, those that can be raised only within its own distinctive conceptual apparatus. Psychologists, sociologists or philosophers faced with any matter of practical policy on, say, the grouping of pupils in schools or the use of punishment, can legitimately comment only on different psychological, sociological or philosophical issues that may be at stake. The disciplines each make their own limited abstractions from the complexities of practice. They tackle no common problems of any kind and none of them is adequate to the proper determining of principles for educational practice. Indeed, there seems an inevitable gap between the conceptual framework within which the issues of practice arise and the conceptual frameworks the distinct disciplines employ for their particular purposes. In seeking to characterise the relationship between the disciplines and the principles of educational theory, I have from the start referred to the disciplines as providing reasons, of many different kinds, for the principles. In this the disciplines are seen to be crucial for the justification of what is claimed in the theory. But how can such diverse, partial and limited theoretical studies ever provide a satisfactory justification for any set of practical principles? Even if the account I have given to date is satisfactory as far as it goes, it is certainly in need of further development.

In these early accounts of the nature of theory, uncertainty about what more might be said led to ambiguities that I now consider can be removed, at least to some significant extent. In particular, my view that the disciplines can provide justification for practical principles which in their turn justify particular educational activities in individual circumstances was interpreted by some in very simplistic ways that must surely be rejected. Taken as giving a methodology for developing rational educational practice, it is clear that this scheme, of proceeding from disciplines to principles to particular activities, simply will not work. As has already been indicated, the disciplines we have deal with certain aspects abstracted from complex practical situations, dealing with these in dissociation from each other. There is no reason whatever to suppose that these abstractions when put together begin to give any adequate understanding of the situation for practical purposes, nor even that they ever could. What other new disciplines might come to contribute to our understanding we cannot at present know, but further, we are not able to see how such an array of disciplines can provide a comprehensive base for the determination of practical principles. It is not just that at present the disciplines we have are too undeveloped and full of disputes for such a method of developing principles to be workable, true though that is. It is rather that the very character of the disciplines seems such that they must prove inadequate as a basis for practical principles.

This approach is in fact simply one version of what Karl Popper labelled Utopian social engineering[7] and is open to all the criticisms he voiced. It sees rational action as action decided on in separation from immediate experience and concrete situations, and then executed in particular circumstances. In this it assumes either that we can achieve a 'clean slate' on which we can write what we want or that we can achieve what we want no matter what the existing state of affairs. Such a degree of control over men and complex social circumstances is, however, quite illusory and the consequences of practical actions of any complexity are always in part unpredictable. For that reason alone this approach always tends in practice to the seeking of ever larger areas of planning and ever more determined efforts to control matters over longer periods of time. But the greater the scale of operation, the greater the scale of the unpredictable and the possible irrationality of the outcome. Popper himself advocated instead what he called piecemeal social engineering, in which we confine ourselves to small-scale operations where there are acknowledged deficiencies in our society. In such circumstances we can more readily adjust matters if things go wrong. Larger-scale changes can be made in the light of more modest experiments on a trial and error basis.

Yet for all his opposition to large-scale rationalism, Popper retains a sophisticated version of the same rationalist theory of action. Individuals act rationally to the extent that they understand each problem and respond to it in the terms it itself presents. A person's grasp of a problem is set in part by his society's institutions and traditions, but there is nothing here that is in principle incapable of being understood in the social and other sciences. (There may be unintended consequences to any rational action, but these too are capable of explanation in scientific terms.) My earlier criticisms question whether such rationalism is in principle possible even on a piecemeal scale. Does a practical situation present itself in terms that can be adequately understood from without, using the necessary disciplines? Or is its character determined much more subtly by factors that can only be understood by the practitioner from within this element of the life of the relevant society, with its institutions, traditions, beliefs and values? If, following Popper, educational theory is not to be seen as a form of Utopian social engineering, it is not clear that his picture of piecemeal social engineering is a correct account either. Maybe his idea of social engineering itself, whatever its scale, needs to be questioned because of the technological model it employs. It is far from obvious that in determining social issues the relationship between knowledge and rational action is the same as that which holds in determining engineering practices. In engineering, rational practice comes from an understanding that conforms to what is the case independently of human beings in a particular society's social system. In education, rational practice must be achieved within an understanding which itself both determines and is determined by the society in which it takes place.[8]

The idea of a methodology moving from the disciplines of educational study to practical principles and then to particular activities is not only practically unworkable and mistaken in its view of rational action, it also involves a serious confusion of methodology with logic. In his book *Educational Theory and the Preparation of Teachers*[9] John Wilson criticises my original account of educational theory precisely because of its inadequacy as an outline of a methodology for the development of justifiable theory. As he points out, this means that the picture whereby educational theory draws on all the knowledge within the various forms (of knowledge) that is relevant to educational pursuits, but proceeds from there in grappling with practical problems, 'has, in practice to be considerably modified. . . . [In] any actual instance of serious research one has to adopt a quite different strategy. . . . We have to start with clarifying some objective, consider the practical difficulties of achieving it, and pick up whatever empirical knowledge we find to be relevant on the way.'[10] Wilson goes on to outline his own view of the methodology with its progressive emphases on different kinds of knowledge and disciplines. Though I have many questions about Wilson's alternative, my outline is certainly unacceptable as a methodology. Whether or not the pattern for the justification of an individual action is by appeal to principles and thence to the disciplines, it does not follow from this that in developing educational theory one must follow a method of deriving principles from the disciplines. How the most defensible practical principles are best achieved and how any proposed principles are to be justified, are two quite different questions. Questions of methodology are not questions of logic, even if the two are not unrelated. Showing, then, the inadequacy as a methodology for educational theory of what was in fact proposed as an outline of the logic of the theory, does nothing to invalidate that outline. But the question of the validity of the outline of the logic remains and its adequacy as an account of the justification of educational activities needs further examination.

In my comments on Popper's notion of social engineering I indicated that an adequate general account of rational action is necessary if we are to understand the development of defensible educational theory. Without such an account the logic of the theory remains unclear and the character of the methodology that serves that logic must as a consequence remain obscure. Only if we are aware of the nature of rational action in general and the elements that are necessary to it will it be possible to consider adequately the justification of particular actions. What my earlier outline of educational theory failed to do was to take into account certain elements within rational action whose significance for the justification of actions was consequently ignored. Any adequate account of educational theory must, I now consider, reject more firmly than I once saw certain central tenets of rationalism in favour of a more complex theory of rational action.

On the rationalist account, which I now wish to reject explicitly, rational action is seen as necessarily premeditated. Action waits on prior reflection. The justification of any action is therefore a matter of the justification of the prior decision in the light of the beliefs and principles on which it was based. Gilbert Ryle long ago argued against this account in terms of his distinction between 'know how' and 'know that'.[11] Not all forms of intelligent 'know how' presuppose that the person possesses the 'know that' of the relevant principles. In telling examples he pointed out that good cooking came before relevant recipes and that valid deductive arguments were used and known to be valid before their principles were formulated. Rational action can, and in certain respects must, precede rational principles, the latter being the result of reflection on rational actions. That is not to say that principles, once formulated, are not useful in promoting rational action, or that the range of rational action cannot be extended by modifying the principles of such action in specific ways. What is being denied is that an adequate account of rational action in general can be given simply in terms of principles determined prior to action and justified independently of such action.

A distinction similar to Ryle's has been made by Michael Oakeshott in his analysis of all human activities requiring skill of any sort.[12] By means of this distinction he not only builds up further criticism of rationalism, but begins to develop an alternative account of rational action. All activities, he claims, involve two kinds of knowledge. There is, on the one hand, what he calls technical knowledge, a knowledge of rules, techniques and principles that can be formulated comprehensively in propositions, which can be learned, remembered and put into practice. On the other hand there is practical knowledge which exists only in use, which is not reflective and cannot be formulated in rules. Its normal expression is in a practice of some sort, in a customary or traditional way of doing things. These two kinds of knowledge Oakeshott considers distinguishable but inseparable, both being involved in every concrete activity. Together they make any skill or act what it is. He explicitly denies, however, that technical knowledge tells us what to do and practical knowledge how to do it. Even in knowing what to do there is involved not only an element of technical knowledge but one of practical knowledge too. The propositions of technical knowledge could not exist without a practical knowledge of how to decide certain questions. Doing anything, therefore, depends on and exhibits knowing how to do it and only part of that knowledge can subsequently be reduced to propositional technical knowledge. What is more, these propositions are not the cause of the activity, nor are they directly regulative of it. Rules and principles cannot be applied to situations by the exercise of knowledge of another kind, practical knowledge. For practical knowledge is not simply some blind unstructured executive competence that applies rules and principles. Practical knowledge consists of organised abilities to discern, judge and perform that are so rooted in understanding, beliefs, values and attitudes that any

11

abstracted propositional statements of those elements or of rules and principles of practice must be inadequate and partial expressions of what is involved. Practical knowledge is acquired by living within the organised social world to which we belong, structured as it is by institutions and traditions of great variety. In education, as in any other area of activity, we come to understand the activity, its problems and their answers from engagement in the activity itself. We have to penetrate the idiom of the activity by practising it. Then, gradually, by a variety of means, we can improve and extend our knowledge of how to pursue it, analysis of the activity and reflection on its rules and principles having their part to play in that process.

On this view, the justification of any individual educational activity cannot be seen simply in terms of an appeal to a set of practical principles. Not merely, as previously seen, because the very existence of principles presupposes the acceptance of at least some activities as independently justifed. But now because practical principles are seen to be necessarily inadequate even for an understanding of any activity let alone for justifying it. Justification must be seen, in Oakeshott's words,[13] as 'faithfulness to the knowledge we have of how to conduct the specific activity we are engaged in', and that is different from 'faithfulness to the principles or rules of the activity'. We may easily be faithful to the latter whilst losing touch with the activity itself. 'Rational conduct is acting in such a way that the coherence of the idiom of the activity ... is preserved and possibly enhanced.' Rules and principles are only 'abridgments' of the coherence of the activity. And if justification of any activity by approach to principles is inadequate, justification of practical principles by an appeal to academic disciplines is equally called in question. The validity of practical principles must, on this view, stem from their being abstracted from practice, rather than some independent theoretical foundation.

Oakeshott's distinction between technical and practical

knowledge draws attention to the nature of practical principles and their relationship to practices and individual activities in a way that makes my earlier outline of the nature of educational theory much too simple. What is not clear, however, is the extent and the way in which he considers the understanding, beliefs, values, attitudes and principles embedded in activities to be incapable of formulation in propositions. Is it that this whole constellation of elements is just too complex ever to be analysed except partially? Is it that it is too subtle and mysterious ever to be amenable to propositional formulations that are anything but distortions? Is it that practical knowledge demands the structuring of capacities in patterns that are in principle capable of conceptualisation but whose incorporation cannot itself be propositionally described? On all these views, rational practices and activities can only be learnt in the exercise of the capacities. But if non-distorting conceptualisation is, at least in principle, possible, even if only partial in its concerns, individual activities can with increasing conceptualisation be subjected to ever more critical analysis and perhaps even to limited forms of justification. And if that conceptualisation can, at least in principle, be comprehensive then justification of a much more rigorous kind is at least possible.

What Michael Polanyi has had to say about the tacit element in all human undertakings is perhaps illuminating here.[14] In any activity of understanding or doing he distinguishes what we are attending to focally, what is before the mind, and that which is tacitly or implicitly known. We attend from the tacit to the focal, the activity demanding an integration of these elements. All activities involve the use of many clues, beliefs and judgments which we do not attend to or apply, which indeed we cannot attend to in performing the activity. They are necessarily held tacitly on this occasion. It is not, however, that these tacit elements cannot in principle be made explicit and on other occasions be entertained focally, though in then considering them explicitly, other elements of a tacit nature will be involved. But when we attend to a tacit element explicitly, we fail to capture its meaning in the integration process in which it functions tacitly. Using these terms, Oakeshott's practical knowledge can be seen as involving tacit elements of understanding, values and principles which are all, at least in principle, capable of being made explicit and can therefore be made subject to critical evaluation. But the integration of these elements within practical knowledge involves their incorporation into an organisation that is, in Polanyi's view, essentially and necessarily unspecifiable. Nevertheless, though Polanyi holds that in the last analysis all knowledge and practical activity rest on irreducible tacit elements, this does not make knowledge or action a merely subjective matter. He maintains firmly that one always acts from the tacit elements to a focal, public truth claim, performance or action in all domains, and that each can have its own critique. What such a critique has always to recognise is that there is no ultimate certainty in any domain but a commitment to tacit elements at a lower level. In activities like education, the complexity of the elements is greater than in the case of, say, technology, for education operates at a higher level incorporating lower levels of knowledge and skill as tacit elements. The existence of the tacit in higher levels of understanding and activity is not seen as excluding rational criticism in these domains any more than its existence in science excludes such criticism there. What is needed is rather a recognition of the complexities of critique at higher levels.

What these considerations from Ryle, Oakeshott and Polanyi indicate forcefully is that we must reject totally the idea that rational action is a matter of bringing about a state of affairs whose character is fully predetermined and justifiable. We must accept rather a view of reason as of its nature able to provide only a partial explicit characterisation of action even when that action is premeditated. Formal justification of even premeditated action is therefore at its best partial. But we must accept further that our understanding of action is in large measure necessarily derived from an analysis of what is judged to be successful action before we understand, let alone formulate explicitly, the rules of principles that it embodies. Professor Hayek[15] has clearly expressed the general position:

> Man acted before he thought and did not understand before he acted. What we call understanding is in the last resort simply his capacity to respond to his environment with a pattern of actions that helps him persist. . . . 'Learning from experience' . . . is a process not primarily of reasoning but of the observance, spreading, transmission and development of practices which have prevailed because they are successful. . . . .The result of this development will in the first instance not be articulated knowledge but a knowledge which, although it can be described in rules, the individual cannot state in words but is merely able to honour in practice. The mind does not so much make rules as consist of rules of action . . . which it has not made.[16]

But this is not just a phenomenon in the early evolution of understanding. It is a persistent element in all understanding.

> Mind is an adaptation to the natural and social surroundings in which man lives and it has developed in constant interaction with the institutions which determine the structure of society. Mind is as much the product of the social environment in which it has grown up and which it has not made as something that has in turn acted upon and altered these institutions.[17]

Hayek's contention is that in any advanced society like our own there exist both elements of order that have a spontaneous origin and elements whose rules are deliberately made. Whatever their origin, the operation of the rules of order may be 'spontaneous' rather than deliberate.[18] We

15

can endeavour to improve on a system of order by articulating and revising the general rules on which it rests but this can only be done at a general level and improvement cannot be obtained if individuals are deprived of the use of their own understanding of particular circumstances both explicit and tacit.[19] However, attempts at individual piecemeal changes within an existing system will only result in uncontrolled disturbances that can lead to many unforeseeable and undesirable consequences unless they are guided by adherence to certain general principles for the evolution of the system in ways judged desirable as a whole.[20]

In keeping with this view, if we are to develop rational educational practice, it now seems to me we must start from a consideration of current practice, the rules and principles it actually embodies and the knowledge, beliefs and principles that the practitioners employ in both characterising that practice and deciding what ought to be done. The practical discourse in which what is going on can be expressed will have much in common with the discourse of everyday practical activities. It will include particular technical terms, beliefs and principles concerned with specifically educational practices and institutions, but these will be embedded within a much wider general body of discourse. Getting at current practice and policy will necessarily involve articulating accurately the concepts and categories that practitioners use implicitly and explicitly, for it is only from descriptions and principles formulated in these terms that an overt rational critique of practice is possible. Any analysis of educational practice achieved in this way constitutes what I shall call the 'operational educational theory' of those concerned. Such an analysis can of course be undertaken to cover a limited or wide range of educational activities. It can relate these in varying degrees to other, non-educational activities, beliefs and principles. It can be concerned with the practice of, say, an individual, a school or an LEA. Of course, any such explicit analysis is only a partial expression of what occurs. But it sets out elements of practice, belief and principle that are to a greater or lesser degree susceptible to overt rational criticism.

In examining the particular actions or activities of an individual practitioner, critical examination can be made in terms of the understanding of the situation employed, the principles used in deciding what to do, the anticipated consequences of different possibilities, the actual consequences and so on. This may be questioning of the individual's action and judgment in the light of all that he can be seen to bring to the situation, both explicit and implicit, or it may be a challenge to the person's operational educational theory in terms of its coherence or the justification of its elements. The first form of questioning is very much an assessment of performance, of the exercise of know how, and an attempt to make explicit the operational rationale of what was done in the particular case in terms of the practitioner's own general operational theory. How far this critique will be possible will vary in particular cases because of their possible uniqueness in crucial respects. It will also vary according to the personal characteristics of the individual concerned. It must, too, be remembered that the burden of much that has been considered earlier implies that the inability of the practitioner or an outsider to provide a satisfactory explicit rationale for an action or activity is of itself no measure of its success. Nevertheless, it is equally true that judgment and action can be trained to be more adequate in relation to a person's existing knowledge, beliefs, principles and capacities through consideration of the operational rationale of particular incidents.

Consideration of particular actions or activities and their rationale may, however, raise critical consideration of the understanding and principles with which the practitioner in general approaches these situations. The question then is no longer whether particular judgments or actions were the best that could be taken by this practitioner in the circumstances in which the situation arose, but whether the understanding, principles and capacities that he could bring were themselves justifiable. It is with the critique of 'operational educational theory' in this sense that educational theory in its wider sense is concerned. Educational theory is thus directed at more rational educational practice by the continuous attempt to develop operational educational theory composed of elements that are as far as possible rationally defensible. But if this pursuit is not to be misunderstood, the complex character of operational educational theory and its partial characterisation of practice must be kept firmly in mind. In general the concepts employed in operational theory will be those used by practitioners as a result of their formal and informal education, training and socialisation. Many of these concepts will be those of everyday life, developed to capture complex situations and activities as existential wholes, whilst taking for granted a common recognition of their detailed characters and their context. The concepts of specifically educational situations and activities will be of exactly the same character. Much of the understanding within this level of theory will have been developed in the context of immediate practical experience and will be co-terminous with everyday understanding. In particular, many of its operational principles, both explicit and implicit, will be of their nature generalisations from practical experience and have as their justification the results of individual activities and practices. In many characterisations of educational theory, my own included, principles justified in this way have until recently been regarded as at best pragmatic maxims having a first crude and superficial justification in practice that in any rationally developed theory would be replaced by principles with more fundamental, theoretical, justification. That now seems to me a mistake. Rationally defensible practical principles, I suggest, must of their nature stand up to such practical tests and without that are necessarily inadequate. This demand stems from the fact that only principles generated in relation to practical experience and that are operationally tested can begin to do justice to the necessarily complex tacit elements within practice. Indeed, I would now argue that the essence of any practical theory is its concern to develop principles formulated in operationally effective practical discourse that are subjected to practical test.

But if the practical testing of principles of this character is central to all practical theories, including educational theory, we must recognise that neither the formulation nor the testing involved is a self-contained enterprise. The activities and practices of everyday life are developed and modified in a wide context of knowledge, beliefs and values about men and their physical and social context. The very concepts in which our implicit and explicit understanding of practice occurs are tied in with concepts of knowledge and understanding of many kinds. Men have developed knowledge and understanding not only in relation to immediate practice, but in the pursuit of scientific, historical, religious and other forms of explanation. These employ their own conceptual schemes in pursuit of their own forms of rationally defensible claims. The concepts and principles of everyday practice and its discourse become modified progressively in the light of scientific advances, changes in our psychological and sociological understanding, and so on. If practical principles are to be rationally defensible they must therefore be seen to be formulated and tested in ways that incorporate wider beliefs and values that are rationally defensible rather than erroneous. In relation to practical affairs, therefore, it is the job of such disciplines as psychology, sociology and philosophy to provide a context of ever more rationally defensible beliefs and values for the development and practical testing of practical principles.

But if practical discourse is itself limited in its capacity to articulate the principles of practice, the discourses of these other disciplines, which have been developed for other purposes, will of themselves be unable to provide any directly helpful forms of conceptualisation for the promotion of rational practice. Their proper significance is, by virtue of

19

their nature, going to be indirect. Any attempt to derive defensible practical principles from the findings of, say, research psychology, must founder on the gross inadequacy of such findings in relation to the complexities, both implicit and explicit, that characterise practical activities. Any attempt to implement such ill-conceived principles can only serve to distort practice into indefensible activities.

Looked at in these terms, the role of such separate disciplines as, say, sociology of education and philosophy of education within the domain of educational theory as a whole must be the appropriate form of criticism of the sociological and philosophical elements that are significant for the formulation and practical testing of practical principles. It is their job to aid these processes in every way possible. It is not their job to be individually or collectively the basis for the direct formulation of practical principles. In so far as they may suggest forms of practice, these will require reformulation in the light of past practical experience of appropriate kinds if they are to have any serious hope of rational defence through practical testing.

The logic of educational theory I therefore now see as demanding the justification of what is done in any particular case by reference to knowledge, understanding and practical principles, which principles have been subject to the test of practical experience. The knowledge, understanding, practical principles and forms of practical test which are thus appealed to incorporate and make use of elements that are open to rational criticism in various contributory disciplines. The justification of these elements in the disciplines is in principle necessary but not sufficient for the justification of the practical principles. It is therefore as mistaken to think of the practical principles of educational theory being justified by appeal to the disciplines as it is to think that a theory in physics is justified by appeal to the validity of the mathematical system it employs.

The best methodology for the development of rational

educational practice is, I think, in large measure an empirical matter. Though the aim must be in part to develop practical principles justified as far as possible in terms that conform to this logic, the justification of these principles can never be more than a matter of degree. In so far, however, as educational theory has in the past concentrated on the development of the contributory or foundational disciplines within their own terms, it has failed to concentrate on the promotion of more rational operational practical principles and their testing in experience. In recent years there has been much more attention given to practical principles and a concern to get at those operationally effective in current practice. There has as yet been little examination of such principles and their attendant beliefs and values by means of the relevant contributory disciplines. There are, however, signs that this work is now developing.

The testing in experience of such principles is likewise in an embryonic stage. It is a complex process in which major disagreements in values and the undeveloped state of relevant work in the contributory disciplines creates many problems. Nevertheless in a modest and as yet relatively unsophisticated way, numerous curriculum evaluation and development projects have made a beginning. But at present it seems to me not possible to advocate any particular methodology for the development of educational theory.

Though it is perhaps true to say that in curriculum work in particular educational theory has begun to recognise something of the logic I am here defending, that recognition has been largely intuitive. Those writing on curriculum theory have had little to contribute to any general elucidation of these issues. In writings on educational theory as such there have been a number of relevant moves. As early as 1969 Harold Entwistle,[21] in a paper analysing the place of theory in the learning of professional skills, made some significant comments on the place of theory in professional practice as such. In a discussion of Ryle's account of intelligent

21

activity and to some extent Polanyi's work, he stresses the limitations of all theoretical considerations for practice because of the unspecifiable, tacit components at the heart of all practice and the fact that logically, practice is prior to theory. Nevertheless he sees the importance of theory in providing a great deal of contextual understanding necessary to intelligent practice. He recognises too the place of practical maxims derived from reflection on practice and refers to the systematisation of maxims into theory that can result from a great deal of reasoning and practice. Both contextual understanding and principles of practice, some of these acquired by the individual prior to performance, he sees as significant for both successful and justifiable practice. But perhaps because he is concerned with success rather than justification, the crucial logical status of practical principles and the relationship of contributory disciplines to these are never directly considered.

In a collection of papers on *Theory and the Practice of Education*, edited by Anthony Hartnett and Michael Naish,[22] in so far as the editors themselves come clean about the nature of educational theory, they seem willing to subscribe to the notion that ideally it would seek to establish rational practical principles. But they are so concerned about disagreements within the disciplines that would supply much of the knowledge on which principles could be based and seemingly irreconcilable disagreements in the values experienced practitioners hold that they conclude:

> practical educational generalisations of whatever kind are likely to be at best tentative and unreliable. . . . What educational theory is likely to be able to offer those engaged in educational practice is not firm guidance but only suggestions and hints about what might be best done and when and how. There is little, if any, possibility of offering practical generalisations which if followed will solve practitioners' practical problems and ensure successful practice. Where theory is available it will have to be

applied and this will inescapably require initiative from the practitioners.[23]

I find this conclusion disappointing in part because earlier in this collection the editors included an extract from the writings of Dorothy Emmet[24] that begins to outline conditions for the promotion of rational judgments. The editors themselves have, with many appropriate qualifications, also developed these conditions a little further.[25] Their pessimism may also stem from a search for principles that will both guarantee success in practice as well as promote the most justifiable practice. These are not the same thing. But above all they seem not to accept the vast potential of the domain of the everyday discourse of experienced and critical teachers for the generation and justification of practical principles. What is needed to combat their pessimism if the importance of practical principles is accepted, is to elucidate much further the nature of practical discourse and the justification in it of maxims and principles, to pursue much more systematically the justification of principles in relation to practice, and to direct the disciplines much more rigorously to aiding this task.

In his paper 'Theory and Practice'[26] D.I. Lloyd extols the importance for practice of what he calls 'common sense' and the activity of 'reflection'. He refers with approval to the fund of knowledge and understanding of people and situations that common sense contains when that term is understood 'as a counterpart to theory'. It contains too 'the advice of the experienced, the wisdom of the old, the perceptive remarks and insight we associate with particular individuals whose judgment we respect'. With that as a background he stresses the value of reflection in particular cases, standing back from what one is doing without losing the details of the situation and in these terms looking at reasons why one action may be preferable to another employing elements of the disciplines in the process. But he calls in question the importance of theory operating at a general level. What can be said in general he sees as having limited scope, individual cases of the same activity having overlapping elements in common as different 'games' might have, rather than specifiable elements common to them all. With much of this I have, of course, the greatest sympathy. But I find it inadequate in two respects. First, the informality of the process of 'reflection' as Lloyd comments on it fails to communicate the elements of stringent critical appraisal there can be not only of individual judgments but of the understanding, values and practical principles directly employed by practitioners as well as of the many wider presupposed beliefs and values. Lloyd, like Hartnett and Naish, seems to me not to do justice at all to what could even now be achieved if we were more systematic in our efforts. This is linked with my second difficulty: Lloyd's use of the Wittgensteinian analogy of the definition of games for the power of generalisations about educational activities. Though faithfulness to individual situations is a necessary part of every justifiable educational judgment, the analogy used I regard as doing scant justice to the explicit development of many educational practices to cover widely agreed and deliberately institutionalised common enterprises, e.g. those of helping children to learn to read or to understand their physical environment. Whatever the character of practical principles, it seems to me they are of a much tougher generality than Lloyd suggests. I see no reason to be shy or coy about common sense and reflection as offering the key to our understanding of the characteristics of practical theories. After all, the central elements of all other theoretical developments, be they in the sciences, theology or philosophy, can be discerned in common sense concerns, out of which they have historically emerged. What we have to do is to try to articulate more adequately the nature of practical judgments and principles and how they in their turn can be rationally pursued.

I therefore find myself very much more in agreement with the outline of 'actual educational theories' in a paper 'Education as a Socio-Practical Field'[27] by Suzanne de Castell and

Helen Freeman. They comment on Lloyd's distinction between reflection and theory (as understood in educational psychology and other disciplines) as being more appropriately seen as a distinction between practitioners' theorising and academic theorising, arguing that in any adequate notion of theory for what they call 'the socio-practical field' of education, the two would be merged. It is to them characteristic of an area of practice like education that the problems practitioners must face are particular, and what counts as a problem and its solution is defined by the people in the context. The practitioner's concern is with the solution of a practical problem which provides the reason for what is to be done. They see the tacit elements of practice and the contingencies, especially the social circumstances, which constrain action as necessary features which any appropriate theory for practice must accept. Such theory, they conclude, must be developed by practising theoreticians. They suggest that any theory will have to take certain basic concepts as given for its purpose (though these concepts could in their turn be questioned in another theory) and that it will contain empirical data and theoretical explanation from the disciplines together with what, in Lloyd's sense, can be referred to as common sense. What is more, such theories will seek to be as unified and coherent as possible. The relationship between theory and practice they see as dialectical, the approach to individual problems being essentially pragmatic.

My major difficulty with this account is that it still seems to me to give inadequate weight to the need to seek the establishment of general principles in what I have labelled practical discourse. The authors stress admirably the need for philosophers of education, educational psychologists and others to be practitioners themselves so that their contributions to educational theory will be developed in relation to the concrete practices and the concepts and beliefs that practitioners employ. Yet the activity of such specialists, for all its practical anchorage, will remain distorting if their contribution is directly allowed to modify practical principles rather than being used in the development of new principles in the dialectical relationship between principles and practice. Practical theory constitutes a domain generated in relationship to practice, using the achievements of the disciplines. In adequately developed theory the effect of the disciplines in practice is to be discerned through the filter of practical principles. It is the justification of individual judgments in relation to general principles and the justification of those principles in relation to individual judgments that is the key to our understanding the logic of educational theory.

Since my article in 1966 for the volume edited by Professor Tibble, the characterisation of the nature of educational principles and their justification has emerged as far more problematical than I then recognised. The significance of the tacit elements in all action can now be seen to be fundamental to any adequate account of practice and its principles. Likewise, the fact that we are ourselves products of the social situations we have created and that our understanding of these situations is central to their being what they are means that the practitioner's view of what is occurring must be recognised as central. These features can to some extent be discerned progressively in writing on educational theory, in certain exploratory approaches within educational research and in new emphases within the teaching of educational studies. There has come to be a focus on the actual practices of education and the discourse practitioners use. It is not so much that what I wrote in 1966 was mistaken as that what I omitted led to a distorting emphasis. Educational theory I still see as concerned with determining rationally defensible principles for educational practice. The adequate formulation and defence of these principles I now see as resting not simply on appeal to the disciplines, but on a complex pragmatic process that uses its own appropriate practical discourse. How best we might give an account of the logic of such discourse and its principles remains I think uncertain, though I have indicated how I think we should approach the matter.

Perhaps the most promising discussions of this now focal question are to be found quite outside the particular context of educational theory, in the contemporary study of critical theory, particularly the work of Habermas and his critics. Habermas has sought to outline the fundamental framework within which rational practical discourse can take place by articulating the basic presuppositions of speech acts. This sets out certain normative conditions for rational decisions and consensus. His approach in formulating these principles that underlie all practical activities can also be used in the context of more particular areas. As one of his most able expositors and critics, Thomas McCarthy, has expressed it:

> As Habermas sees it, the basic idea behind this approach is that speaking and acting subjects know how to achieve, accomplish, perform, produce a variety of things without explicitly adverting to, or being able to give an explicit account of, the structures, rules, criteria, schemata on which their performances are based. The aim of rational reconstruction is precisely to render explicit the structures and rules underlying much 'practically mastered, pre-theoretical know-how', the tacit knowledge that represents the subject's competence in a given domain . . . if the tacit, pre-theoretical knowledge that is to be reconstructed represents a universal know-how . . . our task is the reconstruction of a 'species competence.' Adopting this approach, Habermas advances a proposal for a universal or formal pragmatics.[28]

In another passage he writes:

> Communication that is oriented towards reaching understanding inevitably involves reciprocal raising and recognition of validity claims. Claims to truth and rightness, if radically challenged, can be redeemed only through argumentative discourse leading to rationally motivated consensus. Universal-pragmatic analysis of the conditions of discourse and rational consensus show these to rest on the

supposition of an 'ideal speech situation' characterised by an effective equality of chances to assume dialogue roles.[29]

There is much dispute about many features of Habermas's programme. Whether or not his particular exposition of the ethics of speech acts is correct, and this is far from obvious, it is by no means clear that such an ethic is in any ultimate sense the necessary foundation of rational practice. And just what the implementation of such an ethic means logically and methodologically in the rational critique of more specific practices like those of education, it is not easy to envisage. However, it certainly suggests self-critical, reflective and reconstructive analysis and judgment by different groups of practitioners, operating at different and progressively more deep and wide-ranging levels of presupposition, using the disciplines to maximum degree. That kind of activity, whatever particular form it may come to take, can hardly fail to contribute illuminatingly to rational educational practice. And if practice does indeed precede theory in this area as in others, perhaps this will in due course bring us further understanding of educational theory. Certainly, at present it seems to me to afford us the most hope.

Notes

1 P.H. Hirst, 'Educational Theory', in J.W. Tibble (ed.), *The Study of Education*, London, Routledge & Kegan Paul, 1966.
2 D.J. O'Connor, *An Introduction to the Philosophy of Education*, London, Routledge & Kegan Paul, 1957.
3 Ibid., p. 75.
4 Ibid., p. 76.
5 Ibid., p. 110.
6 G. Langford and D.J. O'Connor (eds), *New Essays in the Philosophy of Education*, London, Routledge & Kegan Paul, 1973, Papers 3 and 4.
7 K. Popper, *The Open Society and Its Enemies*, London, Routledge & Kegan Paul, 1945. Especially vol. 1, ch. 9.
8 For a further criticism of Popper's position, see A. O'Hear, *Karl Popper*, London, Routledge & Kegan Paul, 1980, ch. 8.

9 J. Wilson, *Educational Theories and the Preparation of Teachers*, Slough, NFER, 1975.
10 Ibid., p. 62.
11 G. Ryle, *The Concept of Mind*, London, Hutchinson, 1949.
12 M. Oakeshott, *Rationalism in Politics*, London, Methuen, 1962. See the papers 'Rationalism in Politics' and 'Rational Conduct'.
13 Ibid., pp. 101–2.
14 See particularly, M. Polanyi and H. Prosch, *Meaning*, University of Chicago Press, 1975.
15 F.A. Hayek, *Law Legislation and Liberty*, vol. 1, London, Routledge & Kegan Paul, 1973.
16 Ibid., p. 18.
17 Ibid., p. 17.
18 Ibid., pp. 45–6.
19 See ibid., p. 51.
20 See ibid., p. 60.
21 H. Entwistle, 'Practical and Theoretical Learning', *British Journal of Educational Studies*, vol. 17, nd. 2, 1969.
22 A. Hartnett and M. Naish (eds), *Theory and the Practice of Education*, vol. I, London, Heinemann, 1976.
23 Ibid., p. 121.
24 D. Emmet, *Rules, Roles and Relations*, London, Macmillan, 1966, ch. 9.
25 Hartnett and Naish (eds), op. cit., pp. 100–7.
26 D.I. Lloyd, 'Theory and Practice', *Proceedings of the Philosophy of Education Society of Great Britain*, vol. X, July 1976.
27 S. de Castell and H. Freeman, 'Education as a Socio-Practical Field', *Journal of Philosophy of Education*, vol. 12, 1978.
28 T. McCarthy, 'Rationality and Relativism', in J.B. Thompson and D. Held (eds), *Habermas – Critical Debates*, London, Macmillan, 1982, p. 60.
29 Quoted in Thompson and Held (eds), op. cit., pp. 255–6.

2 Philosophy of education[1]

Richard S. Peters

In this paper I am concerned to give an account of what has
happened to philosophy of education in Great Britain during
the past two decades, to give a brief résumé of its main
controversies, and to ruminate on what directions I think it
should take.

It is generally agreed that in the 1960s and 1970s philosophy of education in Great Britain developed a new look
and was firmly put on the map as a branch of educational
theory. It was sufficiently well established by 1965 for the
Philosophy of Education Society of Great Britain to be
founded with its own journal. Before then philosophy of
education had been unco-ordinated and variously interpreted.
There was, first of all, the pattern adopted by many working
at it in American Colleges of Education, who were determined
to convince their colleagues in the Faculties of Arts that they
were genuinely doing philosophy. They intended to take
schools of thought such as Idealism, Realism, Pragmatism and
to probe their implications for education. Indeed, when I was
first introduced to the subject, the most widely canvassed
question was that of the 'implications' of philosophy for
education. An exception to this were the followers of Dewey
and Kilpatrick whose cohesive pragmatic approach was still
influential. Dewey, in my view, approached philosophy of
education in the right sort of way – via the problems of

education. There was thus no question of the 'relevance' of philosophy. But not everyone, to put it mildly, found his answers acceptable. Indeed, one eminent American philosopher told me wryly, when I was trying to interest him in it, that Dewey set the subject up – and killed it stone dead!

More typical of Great Britain was the Great Educator's approach. Most colleges of education took students on a guided tour of thinkers from Plato to Dewey and valiantly tried to relate their thought to current educational problems. The courses were taught mainly by historians and, indeed, few of the thinkers studied were worth studying for the philosophical content of their thought. There is no question, of course, that a knowledge of the thought of at least some of these thinkers should be part of the heritage into which every teacher should be initiated at some stage of his or her career. But there were three flaws in this approach. Firstly, as taught, the courses were only minimally philosophical. Secondly, the ideas of the great educators were too often extracted from their writings without giving students any training in the form of thought necessary for the assessment of their ideas. Little idea of their historical context, which could be contrasted with modern conditions to which they were applied, was supplied either. *Plato Today* has to be very skilfully contrived to be effective. Thirdly, as the courses were not in the main imaginatively conceived, students found difficulty in grasping their relevance to the pressing problems with which they were faced in the classroom.

Finally, there was what might be called 'principles of education' which are well represented by classics such as Whitehead's *Aims of Education*. At their best they consisted in wisdom and aphorisms about education. Courses of this sort bore witness to the religious foundations of many colleges. They dealt with ethical and spiritual aspects of education which were recognised as not being the province of the psychologist or historian. As a matter of fact, however, such courses included empirical speculation – e.g. Whitehead's famous stages of romance, precision, and generalisation and Sir Percy Nunn's adaptation of the 'hormic' point of view in psychology, which he took from McDougall. This was no accident: for any general maxim such as 'primary school children ought not to be punished' must include both ethical and psychological components. They are, logically speaking, hybrids. In my view it is a very important task of philosophy of education to help to formulate such principles, but, because of their empirical element, it cannot do so on its own. To call 'principles of education' philosophy of education is to make a takeover bid for the philosopher as a kind of oracle.

A departure in England from these three approaches was that of Louis Arnaud Reid who had made his name in aesthetics and who was invited to the University of London Institute of Education to take up a chair in the philosophy of education. He did some imaginative groundwork by setting up the subject as the application of philosophy proper to educational problems. He favoured a synthetic approach and prepared the way for the great change that was to come about in the 1960s when a few people trained in contemporary analytic philosophy moved into the subject and attempted to apply philosophy of a more analytic type to educational problems. This generated a lot of excitement and enthusiasm in the early stages, as existing philosophical critiques of issues surrounding freedom, punishment, authority, knowledge, etc., were applied to education. There was also a growing sense of achievement as work grew on concepts such as 'education', 'learning', 'creativity', 'teaching', 'indoctrination', etc., which had scarcely been touched on at all systematically by 'pure' philosophers.

These pioneers had two general objectives. On the one hand, they were determined that philosophy of education should be genuine philosophy and recognised as such. They were anxious to avoid the American situation in which there is little contact between philosophy of education and 'pure' philosophy. On the other hand, they were determined that philosophy of education should have its feet firmly in schools and should be recognised by teachers as relevant to their work.

The subject, so it now seems to me, was stimulated into life by this initial rush of philosophical blood to the head, but then its arteries began to harden. It settled down to a rather pedestrian period of tidying up and trying to improve on existing analyses and arguments. Few fresh ideas came in from philosophy or from elsewhere. It is amazing, for instance, that only one writer has introduced ideas taken from John Rawls's *A Theory of Justice*.[2] Perhaps, too, the analytic emphasis brought with it a rather narrow, piecemeal approach. Unlike Dewey's philosophy of education, it operated without an explicit theory of human nature, although concepts such as 'reason', 'autonomy', 'needs', 'interests' and 'learning' were confidently tackled, they drifted on the surface with no general account of man and his place in the natural world and social order to anchor them.

However, that is to anticipate. Let us begin at the beginning with a little history. Credit for initiation of this new approach is usually given to C.D. Hardie, who as long ago as 1942 produced his *Truth and Fallacy in Educational Theory*[3] in which he applied techniques learnt from Moore and Broad to the educational theories of motivation, Herbart, and Dewey and to problems of educational theory and measurement. D.J. O'Connor's *An Introduction to the Philosophy of Education*,[4] with a strongly positivistic approach, appeared on the scene in 1957. But perhaps the most decisive event was the establishment, soon after the Second World War, of a chair in the subject at the University of London Institute of Education. Its first occupant was Professor L.A. Reid who got philosophy of education off to a sensitive start. I came on the scene in 1962, having previously spent a period with Israel Scheffler at Harvard, who was pioneering the analytic approach in the USA. I inherited from Reid a small department, including Paul Hirst. The development of outside events encouraged expansion and a more aggressive assertion of the new approach. The events were the expansion of teacher education and the advent of the three-year course and later a fourth year for the BEd.

In 1964 the DES and ATCDE called a conference at Hull to discuss the future of educational studies and I was able there to outline the new approach to philosophy of educa-tion.[5] (This was repeated in my contribution to the Tibble volume, *The Study of Education*,[6] in 1966.) The thesis was that the starting point should be educational problems and that, in particular, ethics, social philosophy, theory of knowledge and philosophy of mind, should be employed, along with other foundation disciplines, such as psychology and sociology, to tackle them. Those working in the philo-sophy of education were excited by the vista of virgin fields that were wide open for work. In the Preface to *Ethics and Education*[7] in 1965 I claimed that 'It will only develop as a rigorous field of study if a few philosophers are prepared to plough premature furrows that run more or less in the right direction.' The 1960s were a period of enthusiasm; there was optimism for what educational theory could achieve. Also there were job prospects in studying philosophy of education and many able people from the teaching profession were recruited to its ranks.

We then had the James Report with its unsympathetic attitude towards educational theory, and the subsequent con-traction of the colleges. Now we have the emphasis on preparation for work in schools and the concentration on basic standards of literacy and numeracy and the problems of immigrants and the handicapped. So LEAs tend to favour practical courses for secondment, and if teachers come to study philosophy of education, they know that they are likely to return to their schools rather than obtain a post in teaching it; for such openings are almost non-existent. In a way this is no bad thing, for if philosophy of education has any value this should be apparent in the transformation which it brings about in a teacher's outlook and in the more critical appraisal which it encourages of the school situation.

It is not meant to be an exit permit from schools to a more reflective type of life in a college or university. But from the point of view of philosophy of education these trends have meant a period of consolidation – some would say a struggle for survival.

Nevertheless, philosophy of education still survives. There are over 500 members of the Philosophy of Education Society of Great Britain and *The Journal of Philosophy of Education* sold over 1,000 copies last year. Will the subject continue to flourish? When, in 1975, I resigned the chairmanship of the Society after ten years of office, I argued that the subject was at rather a scholastic stage, tidying up minutiae of previous analyses and arguments. To advance it must both become more philosophical and get itself more deeply involved in current practical problems. Whether it is developing in either of these directions will emerge as I proceed.

On the question of its philosophical standing, I think it can be said that it has established itself as a respectable, if lowly, branch of philosophy. Eminent philosophers have interested themselves in it such as Gilbert Ryle, Michael Oakeshott, David Hamlyn, Roy Edgley, Anthony Flew, Anthony Quinton, Richard Hare, Dan O'Connor, Bernard Williams, Mary Warnock, Martin Hollis, Godfrey Vesey, A. Phillips Griffiths and in 1973 a special conference on philosophy of education was organised by the Royal Institute of Philosophy at Exeter.[8] In the early 1970s I was asked to produce a book on philosophy of education for the OUP Readings in Philosophy series.[9] The International Library of Philosophy of Education already contains over a dozen volumes. Philosophy of education now appears as an option in the philosophy programmes of many philosophy departments, and it is no longer regarded, as it used to be twenty years ago, as not proper philosophy.

It is impossible to gauge the standing of the subject in the eyes of those concerned with the detailed work of schools. There is no doubt that, during the progressive hey-day of the 1960s, culminating in the Plowden Report, it made an impact, if an adverse one, in many quarters. For the analytic approach was brought to bear on some of the slogans of progressivism such as 'growth', 'the needs and interests' of the child, and 'learning by discovery'. *Perspectives on Plowden*,[10] which I edited, created quite a furore, and Robert Dearden's *The Philosophy of Primary Education*,[11] for all its cautious sanity and clarity, was regarded by many as a seditious tract. In a way it was a pity that philosophy of education was brought forcibly to the attention of teachers in this way; for they assumed that, as it was critical of some of the tenets of child-centred education, it must be traditional in its allegiance. This was a completely false reading of the position underlying the criticisms. Indeed, *The Logic of Education*,[12] which I wrote a little later with Paul Hirst, was an explicit attempt to steer a middle way between the traditional and child-centred approaches. To my knowledge no philosophers of education contributed to the Black Papers!

1 The London line

Most people who speak of the subject will remark wryly that at least during the 1965–75 decade philosophy of education was dominated by the 'London line' described somewhat whimsically by Bernard Williams as the 'khaki regulars from Malet Street'. There is some truth in this in spite of major differences between London philosophers; but it is not surprising because of the size of the London department, which is the biggest in the world, and the fact that a large percentage of British philosophers of education were trained in London. Also I, like Scheffler in America, came from a philosophy department and shared his conviction that analytic philosophy, which was the currently accepted orthodoxy, had much to offer to education. So there was the authority of an established discipline behind the work. The result was that much of the writing during the past decade has consisted in developing or attacking ideas emanating from this school of thought.

The so-called 'London line' had two main strands to it – an ethical and social one provided by myself and an epistemological one provided by Paul Hirst. In my *Ethics and Education*[13] I attempted, in too much of a hurry, to tackle the main points where education impinges on ethics and social philosophy. My thesis was that the democratic way of life is based on discussion and the use of practical reason and that this is to be interpreted as a social activity presupposing the principles of impartiality, respect for persons' freedom, and the consideration of interests. These principles can be justified, I argued, by transcendental arguments. I employed this ethical apparatus to deal with the educational implementation of equality, freedom, authority, punishment, and democracy. Unfortunately, this basic thesis, which I still think defensible, was flawed by two major mistakes. Firstly, a too specific concept of 'education' was used which concentrated on its connection and understanding. Secondly, I tried but failed to give a convincing transcendental justification of 'worthwhile activities', such as science or agriculture as distinct from Bingo or playing fruit machines, which I thought relevant to the curriculum. (Actually, my later books *Psychology and Ethical Development*[14] and *Education and the Education of Teachers*[15] contained some better work. But they were collections of articles and did not make the same impact. It was *Ethics and Education* that attracted the academic flak.) I have now come to see that I was trying to extract too much from the concept of education, which is more indeterminate than I used to think. The end or ends towards which processes of learning are seen as developing, e.g. the development of reason which we stressed so much are aims of education, not part of the concept of 'education' itself and will depend on acceptance or rejection of the values of the society in which it takes place. I have recently written a paper trying to work this out in the case of democratic societies, where the development of reason has its natural home.[16]

Hirst's contribution was very different. It was largely based on his seminal paper 'Liberal Education and the Nature of Knowledge'[17] which was reprinted in several collections and developed in subsequent articles. He was in part stimulated by Louis Arnaud Reid's *Ways of Knowledge and Experience*[18] and attempted to apply this approach in more precise terms to the curriculum. His thesis was that education was the development of the 'rational mind' and that the curriculum should be based fairly and squarely on the nature of knowledge, which could be divided into seven or eight 'forms', the basis of division being types of fundamental concepts employed, truth criteria, and methods of testing. 'Forms' of knowledge could be combined in 'fields' such as geography or classics and it was a matter for the teacher whether or not to try to 'integrate' them in a topic-centred approach or to teach them on their own. Hirst also wrote a very clear and forceful article on 'What is Teaching?'[19]

It might be asked why this alliance between myself and Hirst developed so that we eventually wrote *The Logic of Education* together, apart from reasons of proximity. The answer is that we both believed strongly in the values of reason and that I was sympathetic to Hirst's approach because in ethics as well as in science, I had for a long time distinguished the mode of experience, characterised by distinctive principles and attitudes, from the content which had been developed by it and which was constantly being tested and revised by recourse to it. Thus though I was always unhappy about calling some of Hirst's forms forms of knowledge, and often substituted 'modes of experience', I was sympathetic to the general approach. The partnership was sundered by Hirst's departure to Cambridge in the early 1970s.

What is one to say about it as a phenomenon? Well it certainly gave philosophy of education a vigorous lead and did much to establish it as a branch both of philosophy and of educational theory. Chairs in education have been obtained by several people who either taught or trained in the London department – Paul Hirst at King's College, London, and at the

Cambridge Department of Education, Leslie Perry at the University of Warwick and at King's College, London, Ray Elliott and Robert Dearden at the University of Birmingham, Hugh Sockett at the New University of Ulster and now at the University of East Anglia, and Richard Pring at the University of Exeter. The 'London line' contained mistakes, but these were clearly enough presented to be seen as mistakes and so helped to develop critical debate and the clarification of various problems arising from it. The question is whether its declining ascendancy has left a vacuum. Certainly no new 'paradigm' has displaced it. But are there any signs of new trends developing which will carry the subject forward? A more detailed look at the state of the subject may help to answer that question.

2 Philosophy of education and educational theory

One of the recurring debates has been on the nature of educational theory itself and the relation of philosophy of education to it. O'Connor wished to reserve the term 'theory' for those educational studies that are testable by observation. Of course, value judgments, historical knowledge, etc., are relevant to education, but are not to be regarded as part of educational theory in a strict sense.[20] Hirst, on the other hand, claimed that educational theory is to be conceived not as scientific theory, but as the complement of practice – a body of precepts and generalisations that guide actions of various sorts. On this view, studies like ethics and history would be as much part of educational theory as the empirical disciplines.[21] On the whole, Hirst's view has been accepted by philosophers of education but they have continued debating about the precise relation of theory to practice.[22]

In Hirst's view, ideally psychologists, philosophers, sociologists, etc. should get together and bring their disciplines to bear in relation to some educational problem of practice so that precepts could be formulated for dealing with it. In actual fact almost no projects have been set up like this. The exception is the work of the Farmington Trust on moral education.[23] The conceptual framework was set up at considerable length and problems identified for investigation. But the team was disbanded before the investigations could get under way. The main reason for the dearth of this type of approach is that, when from 1964 onwards, the so-called foundation disciplines became explicitly differentiated from each other in the attempt to rest the rather woolly study of education on a more rigorous basis, the disciplines tended to go their own way and to pay little attention to each other unless they happened on something that could be criticised. The institutionalisation of educational theory has to a large extent determined its disintegrated character.

This conception of the relation of theory to practice should not, however, be conceived of as just being geared to the solution of particular problems. There is also the whole sphere of policy and of how situations are conceived. In the sphere of policy two interdisciplinary books which I edited, namely *Perspectives on Plowden*[24] and *The Role of the Head*,[25] were directed towards making people think about current issues from different points of view, rather than at putting forward solutions to problems. And the vast amount of literature from psychologists attacking the IQ, and from sociologists illustrating the social basis and consequences of the tripartite system, was highly influential in the move towards comprehensivisation. The student of educational theory too often expects it to provide recipes that can be applied in school the next day, and much of the writing about educational theory encourages this picture of it. In my view little of educational theory is as closely related to practice as this – e.g. the teaching of skills. More of it has the function of transforming a person's outlook so that a classroom situation is viewed in a different light and the stereotypes which live on from the past are shaken and perhaps shattered.

As far as philosophy of education goes, not all work done

has been isolated from other disciplines. In the field of learning, for instance, there was an Aristotelian Society symposium on the subject of whether learning implies knowledge,[26] which was followed up by papers on the same theme. This was largely analytical philosophy of the usual sort relying on the analysis of ordinary language and common-sense assumptions. But there was also Hamlyn's work in which a theory emerged from a constructive critique of the work of Piaget and Chomsky.[27] Similarly, there has been a certain amount done in moral education in the usual style of moral philosophy,[28] but I myself have done a lot of work constructing a viewpoint out of a critique of the Piaget–Kohlberg theory.[29]

A strange absence of interdisciplinary work, which might have been done by philosophers of education, was evident in the muted response to the sociology of knowledge movement which was launched by M.F.D. Young's *Knowledge and Control.*[30] There was Richard Pring's spirited reply, 'Knowledge out of Control',[31] and a dialogue between Michael Young and John White[32] in which, to put it mildly, there was very little meeting of minds, but it was left to the 'pure' philosophers Anthony Flew[33] and Mary Warnock[34] to mount a more measured attack on the position. Maybe most philosophers of education thought the position too confused to be worth disentangling. But, nevertheless, an opportunity was missed for tackling important problems that lie between the two subjects.

3 Education and teaching

The concept of 'education' has, needless to say, received plenty of attention. Roughly speaking attempts to give an account of it have been either too specific or not specific enough. I linked it too closely with knowledge and understanding and Downie, Telfer and Loudfoot[35] coined a term 'educativeness' as the intrinsic end of education which was

41

equivalent to the possession of various types of knowledge. Such analyses put attitudes, emotions, wants and actions in an awkward position and raise queries about aesthetic and religious experience. On the other hand, Langford,[36] who equated education with becoming a person, was not specific enough. For adult education thrives and those who attend schools and colleges in order to be educated, are surely persons already. Mary Warnock,[37] in despair at the elusiveness of the concept, said that it is quite good fun to attempt an analysis of 'education' but that it is used in too many ways to be profitable. Nevertheless she committed herself to two views about it, both of which are eminently disputable, namely that it stops at a given time and that it is to be seen just as a preparation for life. John Dewey would turn in his grave if such confident assertions reached him! Hartnell and Naish,[38] following Gallie,[39] claimed that 'education' is an essentially contested concept and will be used in different ways according to people's ideologies. There is some truth in this; for it is common practice to incorporate aims into the concept of education and aims are certainly contestable.

The question is, however, whether there are any incontestable things that can be said about 'education' and whether the point can be located at which contestability arises. For instance, it is surely contestable that education involves some kind of systematic learning or development. Secondly, it has now been distinguished from training which is used for learning directed towards some specific end. By contrast, education is concerned with the sort of learning that a person requires *qua* person and not just in some specific capacity. It will consist in the development of those forms of awareness and skills which he will require generally in facing the various facets of the human condition in the natural, interpersonal, and socio-economic worlds which he has to inhabit. It is at this point that contestability enters in; for various forms of learning and development tend to be emphasised as aims. And these will depend on the society in which a person is nurtured and the ethical and social philosophies prevalent. Is he to be viewed primarily as a citizen or as an individual seeking his own fulfilment? Is autonomy to be encouraged or conformity to tradition? Is the bias of his awareness to be towards scientific or aesthetic forms of awareness? How is education related to preparation for an occupation?

In philosophy of education aims tend to be formulated in rather an *ad hoc* way. Mary Warnock, for instance, produced virtue, the imagination, and work.[40] But why just these three? Autonomy is frequently cited as an aim without any supporting rationale from a theory of human nature or an ethical standpoint. The exception is Hare, whose adherence to autonomy derives from a well-worked out, if controversial, ethical position.[41] Creativity has been another favourite, but little background to it has been filled in except by Elliott in his outstanding article on the subject.[42] My point is really a two-fold one. Firstly, conceptual analysis has tended to be too self-contained an exercise. Criteria for a concept are sought in the usage of the term without enough attention being paid to the historical or social background and view of human nature which it presupposes. Secondly, if something is put forward as an aim, a justification both for it and its emphasis is required. An interesting historical venture into the richer type of analysis which I am advocating was given by John White[43] in his article showing how the highly individualistic aim of 'the self-realisation of the individual' was a pale legacy of the more communitarian idealist tradition.

Another example of the unsatisfactoriness of self-contained analyses was the debate about the concept of 'teaching'. Hirst, in the article already mentioned, stressed the intention to bring about learning, which was adapted to the•cognitive state of the learner by use of various acts by means of which attention was drawn to content to be learned. Freeman[44] argued that 'teaching' is only properly used when learning actually occurs. If someone 'teaches' and no one learns, he is trying to teach. Now usage supports either thesis. A believer in usage can argue that we can ask whether spelling is taught

43

or caught; Freeman can reply that we can say that all a tutor taught his pupils was his mannerisms. And to both it could be said that more needs to be said about acts. Otherwise conscientious librarians, who hand out books, so that students can learn, are teaching. And this is the sort of impasse that so often faces this sort of analysis. But two points need to be made. Firstly, if the teaching is taking place in an educational institution, Hirst's insistence on intention must be right. For it would be unintelligible that teachers would be employed who did not, in general, have the intention that others would learn. How successful they proved to be would be a further question. On the other hand, there is the hidden curriculum, and teachers bring about all sorts of learning that they do not intend. Whether we say that they were 'teaching' such things does not much matter. For the second point is that behind the insistence on using 'teach' in a certain way lie two very different educational policies. Hirst wants clear-cut objectives and teachers using various acts to obtain them. He wants, as it were, to limit teaching to a manageable task. Freeman, on the other hand, wants to widen the responsibility of the teacher, to make him or her more aware of the hidden curriculum and of what pupils actually learn which may not be at all what teachers intend. Again the analysis of the concept must be viewed against a wider background of policy. Concepts cannot be dealt with in an abstract and isolated way. They have a social and historical context which must be taken into account and analysis of them must have a point related to some educational problem. It would be pointless, for instance, to attempt an analysis of concepts such as 'chalk' or 'desk'. At one time I thought that the concept of 'school' was in this category. But the de-schooling movement has led me to revise my premature judgment!

Just as autonomy has been regarded almost as the supreme virtue by philosophers of education, so threats to it have been regarded as the supreme vices. This has been evident in the considerable literature concerning the 'neutral teacher' and 'indoctrination'. The controversy about the neutral teacher was sparked off by Lawrence Stenhouse's Humanities Project,[45] which, rather absurdly, was directed only towards early school-leavers. He was much concerned that 'relevant' topics such as sex, law and order, and war should be discussed by adolescents, but very alive to the danger of indoctrination if they were. He therefore proposed that material should be prepared for use for teachers and that they should act as neutral chairmen when the material was discussed. They were not to be neutral on procedural matters; they must value truth and take steps to ensure that discussion proceeded along lines relevant to it. But they must not take sides and reveal their views on substantive issues. There was an early debate on the subject between Bailey and Elliott[46] and another one at the Royal Institute of Philosophy Conference at Exeter.[47] The topic was taken up again at the Annual Conference of the Society in 1976.[48] In all these debates it never seemed to me that sufficient attention was paid to the social as distinct from intellectual values of procedure that discussion itself presupposes. The teacher has to ensure freedom of speech, be impartial, and show respect for people putting forward views. He can stand fast on such values and be 'neutral' on issues like gambling and pre-marital sex relations. But how can he be neutral about discriminating against women when impartiality requires that he do his best to make sure that girls in his group are not disregarded on account of their sex?

The background to the neutral teacher controversy was the fear of indoctrination. The trouble, however, was that no one was quite clear what it was. Given that a person who has been indoctrinated holds a fixed body of beliefs in a way that makes him impervious to criticism, the problem was to locate the core of the concept.[49] Is it the intention to bring about this state of mind in another? Must the beliefs be doctrines or can someone be indoctrinated in mathematics? Or are the acts by means of which the state of mind is produced crucial?

To my mind the controversy would have been considerably clarified if what constitutes a 'doctrine' had been more decisively determined and if the acts that are meant to be crucial to the concept had been delineated in more detail.

4 The teaching of particular subjects

One of the surprising gaps in philosophy of education has been the lack of work done on the particular subjects. With the exception of Burston's[50] work on the teaching of history and the odd article on the teaching of Nuffield maths[51] and science,[52] work has been more or less confined to subjects on the defensive in schools, namely PE and RE. Carlisle initiated the PE debate by attempting an aesthetic defence of it.[53] A moral defence was put forward by Aspin.[54] Carr[55] entered the scene with a claim for the virtues of PE in developing practical knowledge – an aspect of life hitherto overlooked by philosophers of education. There has also been an interesting debate on the adjoining topic of competition, Dearden cautiously in favour of it, Fielding vociferously against it.[56]

There have been two main issues in the sphere of religious education. The first is whether it is possible, which revolves round its claims to be a legitimate form of knowledge, whether it is a self-contained 'form of life' and the implications for education of whatever answers one gives to these fundamental questions. Hudson[57] wrote a positive well-rounded article on the subject and there was a symposium at the 1978 annual conference.[58] The second question assumes that it is possible, in some form, and asks what should be done about it in state schools. Most of the literature about this has, of course, been contributed by those in RE.[59] But Paul Hirst also has written an article dealing with this issue.[60]

With the position of religion having become so indeterminate on the curriculum the interest in moral education has grown apace, though whether it should be part of the formal curriculum is hotly debated. John Wilson, whose work with the Farmington Trust has already been mentioned, firmly believes that it should be. Adolescents should be instructed in moral reasoning just as they are in mathematical reasoning. Peter McPhail,[61] too, working for the Schools Council, produced material to be used in schools. But this was directed towards getting young people to feel concern for others rather than towards improving their ability to reason. And in 1977 a conference was organised at Leicester at which Kohlberg from Harvard tried to instruct British teachers in how to use his moral development material in schools. Others, such as Mary Warnock,[62] though strongly in favour of moral education, deprecate its special introduction as a classroom subject. Moral behaviour, to which the example of the teacher and the ethos of the school can contribute much, is to be stressed, rather than a particular mode of reasoning. Of course, moral issues arise and should be discussed in a variety of subjects. But they should not be singled out and discussed specially during two periods a week.

5 The curriculum as a whole

Apart from Hirst's ambitious attempt to answer the most fundamental questions about the curriculum as a whole largely by reference to 'forms of knowledge', there have been few large-scale philosophical approaches to this topic. Hirst's own approach, too, is self-confessedly limited; for he has been concerned with liberal education, and not with vocational and practical subjects. White[63] made rather a Hobbesian sortie into the field; for just as Hobbs started from individual consent and ended up with advocating absolutism, so White started from the subjective preferences of the individual and argued that education should provide him with the equipment to make autonomous choices amongst them. But ingenious argumentation showed that to do so he should be given a compulsory equipment very similar to Hirst's forms of knowledge. Dearden[64] made extensive use of Hirst's forms in sketching a primary curriculum, though he was hostile to the inclusion of religion. Pring,[65] on the other hand, was more critical of Hirst's approach and more worried about the role of common sense and its relation to specialised studies. He was also much concerned about the meaning and desirability of 'integrating' various studies, a subject with which Hirst[66] has also concerned himself. Sockett[67] has concentrated mainly on issues to do with the rational planning of the curriculum. He has tackled the notion of 'objectives', beloved by curriculum planners, and what could be meant by taking means to ends in this context. Finally, there has been Barrow's *Commonsense and the Curriculum*,[68] in which problems of curriculum content are brought down to earth by a robust utilitarianism.

6 Social philosophy and education

It is interesting that though certain parts of *Ethics and Education*, e.g. those on the concept of 'education' and 'worthwhile activities', gave rise to numerous attacks, the main body of the book, which was concerned with social principles, did not stimulate much further discussion. I know of no scrutiny of the concept of authority, for instance. Freedom has attracted little attention save for a symposium on academic freedom at the Exeter conference.[69] There was also a symposium on equality at the same conference[70] and Mary Warnock[71] has recently provided an exhaustive rundown of views on equality and their relevance to education. David Cooper's book, *Illusions of Equality*, written from – avowedly inegalitarian point of view, should prove a stimulating contribution to the subject. He is the first to make extensive use of John Rawls's massive tome on *The Theory of Justice*.[72] Discipline and punishment have been rather brusquely treated by John Wilson[73] and a somewhat offbeat view of punishment was put forward by P.S. Wilson.[74] But little else has happened. Democracy itself has attracted little attention save for one or two discussions on participation and procedures of discussion.[75] On the other hand, new areas have been opened up which were not dealt with in any detail in *Ethics and Education*. Rights in education got under way with a Society symposium.[76] The topic was taken up by many others in the Australian journal *Educational Philosophy and Theory*.[77] Work in political education has also been growing steadily and, like moral education, has now a journal devoted to it. Pat White, beginning with her article on 'Education, Democracy and the Public Interest',[78] has contributed much to this development and in her paper 'Workplace Democracy and Political Education'[79] has even followed Mr Callaghan's advice in the Great Debate that we should relate education more closely to work! Interestingly enough, some of the themes of this debate were anticipated by Sockett,[80] in an article on teacher accountability, and by John White,[81] in another concerned with state control of the curriculum. Mary Warnock,[82] too, had made a plea for work as one of the three aspects of the good life for which education should be a preparation.

7 Future prospects

Having plodded in rather a pedestrian way through work done by British philosophers of education it is now incumbent on me to raise my eyes a bit, to reflect on the past and to ruminate about the future.

(i) The dearth of books

One of the most significant features of the past has been the plethora of articles and collections of articles and the dearth of books, leaving aside small monographs. The only major works, apart from those of 'The London line' and Hamlyn's

Richard S. Peters

Experience and the Growth of Understanding,[83] have been Barrow's *Plato, Utilitarianism and Education*[84] and Mary Warnock's *Schools of Thought*. The former attracted little following because the difficulties inherent in utilitarianism were enhanced by emphasising Plato's concern with happiness; the latter was an eclectic critique of various points of view, but her own thesis that education is a preparation for the good life consisting in virtue, work and the imagination was merely asserted and not argued. There is the highly original work of R.K. Elliott, but this has so far been confined to articles.[85] Also John Wilson's book, *A Preface to Philosophy of Education*, set squarely in the analytic tradition, may prove to be important, though many may be surprised at the number of 'conceptual truths' he discovers about education, learning and the human conditions. There are Marxist critiques issuing from Australia, but it remains to be seen if these will build up into a positive position.

(ii) The need for more philosophical depth

The dearth of books in philosophy of education may be connected with my second point which is the need for more philosophical depth. I have already mentioned the rather *ad hoc* way in which autonomy has been floated off as an aim. But to be convincing it cannot confine itself to the individual's proclivity to deliberate and decide. It requires reference to desires and emotions and a theory of the self which puts it in proper perspective. It requires an account of the type of social relations characteristic of an autonomous person and of the kind of social conditions under which they are possible. It also requires an excursion into ethics and social philosophy to provide a justification for it. The same is true of Hirst's 'forms of knowledge'. They can only be salvaged or sunk by detailed work in epistemology in which the nature of the categorial concepts, that are meant to differentiate the forms, is examined, and more is said about truth criteria in spheres such as aesthetics and religion. Above all philosophy of education is in need of a more explicit theory of human nature. In the past concepts such as 'the rational mind', 'autonomy', 'learning', 'interests', etc. have been treated in too much of a vacuum. The emotional aspect of education has been more or less neglected save by John Wilson[86] and myself.[87] Practical knowledge and skills, together with habits, have received only brief treatment. In the particular sphere of moral education, too, it is the Piaget–Kohlberg cognitive developmental theory, with all its philosophical errors and obscurities, its methodological defects, and its neglect of the effective, that has attracted most attention. Indeed, it has become almost an industry! A more adequate theory must take more account of human nature as a whole as well as of the multi-faceted character of ethical theory. This means giving more attention to the effective side of morals, to will and self-esteem and the social factors which influence development. The emphasis in moral education has been Kantian; it badly needs a Humean corrective. It typifies philosophy of education. Like Rousseau in *Emile*, we have been dealing too much with 'man in the abstract'.[88] This brings me to my third point which is a development in more detail of my present point about the need for a theory of human nature.

(iii) *The need to integrate philosophy with other disciplines*

Philosophy of education is also part of educational theory and can scarcely say anything without recourse to the empirical. The celebrated paradox of freedom, for instance, which is often illustrated by Golding's *The Lord of the Flies*,[89] makes assumptions of a Hobbesian sort about children's nature. Is one justified in advocating a reformative theory of punishment in schools without studying the evidence about its reformative effects? One can discuss endlessly whether learning implies knowledge, whether attitudes are learnt or acquired, etc.; one can demonstrate that people like Piaget have often mistaken logical features of learning for empirical ones. But in putting forward an educational position, in which learning must be central, can one ignore what is known empirically about the general conditions of learning? For it is not all to do with the logic of the subject matter. If psychologists have tended to ignore this in putting forward general theories of learning, have not we been a trifle impatient with their contribution? Hamlyn's *Experience and the Growth of Understanding*, for all its difficulty, is a model of this sort of approach. For he uses a critique of Piaget and Chomsky to develop his own theory. The positive part of the book, however, when he postulates the dependence of concepts and language development on pre-linguistic reactions between parent and child, would have been strengthened had he made reference to recent empirical work done in this area.

It may well be said that specialisation and the proliferation of work in the different educational disciplines do not permit us to proceed as Dewey did in developing a comprehensive theory. This may well be so. But just as what Hamlyn and I have written about learning and moral education takes off from work done by psychologists, so others could explore other areas of contact. Bruner's work, for instance, is wide open for a philosophical critique. It is too much to expect a philosopher of education to master all the literature of another discipline. But it is not too much to expect him to be familiar with an area of it relevant to a problem on which he is working. Without such attempts at synthesis, at least in specific areas, it is difficult to see how educational problems can be adequately tackled. But the ways in which we are trained and institutionalised make it very difficult for us to do more than 'our thing'. My question is whether 'our thing' on its own is enough. Philosophy of education must become more explicitly part of educational theory as well as strengthen its philosophical foundations.

(iv) Need to loosen up the analytic approach

This suggestion that philosophy of education should form a more integral part of educational theory has implications for method. We should not be too wedded to the paradigm of trying to analyse a concept by examining verbal usage. Whatever mileage, for instance, is there in examining the usage of a term like 'curriculum'? In tackling problems we should be more alive to technical as well as to common-sense approaches to them. The important thing is to have a problem. Without this conceptual analysis, or phenomenology, or any other approach, is scholastic. In approaching problems through technical theories as well as through common sense we may well find that, in certain fields, such theories are jargonised ways of stating the obvious. But it is not always so and we should not make premature pronouncements. Philosophy should influence and be influenced by empirical work. Too often, I fear, we stand on the touch-line and jeer when the work is done instead of trying to become participants in it.

(v) Alternative to or revision of 'forms of knowledge' basis for curriculum as a whole needed

Fifthly, somebody must come up with a convincing alternative to Hirst's 'forms of knowledge' thesis as a philosophical foundation to the curriculum – or he must develop his theory in greater detail to meet more adequately important objections to it as it stands. Without such a theory modern discussions of the core curriculum, etc., seem very *ad hoc* – a paradise for gimmickry and sociological speculation.

(vi) Need for more work on philosophy of particular subjects

Sixthly, the field is wide open for work in the philosophies of the particular school subjects. We cannot live for ever on history, religion and physical education.

(vii) More thought needed about concept of 'education'

Seventhly, thought must be given again to the concept of 'education' and its aims which must take more account of human nature and the society in which it operates, and which must also take more seriously, not just Mr Callaghan's demand that education should be related to work, but also that it should be related to leisure; for the new technology will probably make education for leisure as much a problem for the 1980s as education for work has been for the 1970s.

(viii) More sensitivity to contributions coming from outside needed

Eighthly, those working in the subject must be more sensitive to contributions coming from outside. I instanced the muted response to the sociology of knowledge movement which, I think, was a great opportunity lost. Another case in point is the dearth of discussion of the de-schooling movement. I wrote an article influenced by it called 'Dilemmas in Liberal Education'[90] and Robin Barrow has produced a trenchant critique of some romantics like Illich and Reimer in his *Radical Education*.[91] But there is no fair and square facing of the basic question whether schooling itself, as distinct from contingent ways of organising it, is compatible with education.

(ix) The need to relate philosophy of education to practical issues

Finally, at the more practical end Robert Dearden, in his *Problems of Primary Education*,[92] has shown the sort of thing that can be done. There is general treatment of aims, objectives and child-centred education. But there is also more specific treatment of problems of reading, learning by discovery, and the integrated day. More work of this sort could be done on standards, assessment,[93] education in a multicultural society, and further work on the role of the head. With falling school rolls the case for smaller schools could be examined and something might even be done on the philosophy of comprehensive schooling.

Conclusion

Certainly this more low-level, down to earth, type of work is as important to the future of philosophy of education as higher-level theorising. Many would say that it is more important in the present economic climate, but I would dissent from this view; for a recurrent theme of my account of the past has been its piecemeal, rather *ad hoc* character. I do not think that down to earth problems such as the ones which I have mentioned can be adequately or imaginatively dealt with unless the treatment springs from a coherent and explicit philosophical position. The excitement of the 1960s came from exploring uncharted areas of education from a definite, if perhaps deficient standpoint. What we are waiting for is a new standpoint that will perform the same kind of function in the 1980s. What I would like to see would be a development of the 'London line' with more stress on social values and human nature. (There have been countless references to my work on 'Respect for Persons' in *Ethics and Education*, but practically none to my work on 'Fraternity'.) But maybe there will be a 'paradigm shift' and something very different will take its place. But I have simply no idea what this might be. I would hope, however, that the emphasis on clarity, the producing of arguments, and keeping closely in touch with practice remain.

Notes

1 My thanks are due to Paul Hirst for his very helpful comments on an earlier version of this paper.
2 J. Rawls, *A Theory of Justice*, Cambridge, Mass., Harvard University Press, 1971.
3 C.D. Hardie, *Truth and Fallacy in Educational Theory*, Columbia, Teachers' College, 1962.
4 D.J. O'Connor, *An Introduction of the Philosophy of Education*, London, Routledge & Kegan Paul, 1957.
5 R.S. Peters, 'The Place of Philosophy in the Training of Teachers', reprinted in R.S. Peters, *Education and the Education of Teachers*, London, Routledge & Kegan Paul, 1977.
6 J.W. Tibble (ed.), *The Study of Education*, London, Routledge & Kegan Paul, 1966.
7 R.S. Peters, *Ethics and Education*, London, Allen & Unwin, 1966.
8 Published as S.C. Brown (ed.), *Philosophers Discuss Education*, London, Macmillan, 1975.
9 R.S. Peters (ed.), *The Philosophy of Education*, Oxford University Press, 1973.
10 R.S. Peters (ed.), *Perspectives on Plowden*, London, Routledge & Kegan Paul, 1969.
11 R.F. Dearden, *The Philosophy of Primary Education*, London, Routledge & Kegan Paul, 1968.
12 P.H. Hirst and R.S. Peters, *The Logic of Education*, London, Routledge & Kegan Paul, 1970.
13 R.S. Peters, *Ethics and Education*, op. cit.
14 R.S. Peters, *Psychology and Ethical Development*, London, Allen & Unwin, 1974.
15 R.S. Peters, 'The Place of Philosophy . . .', op. cit.
16 R.S. Peters, 'Democratic Values and Educational Aims', *Teacher's College Record*, Feb. 1979.
17 P.H. Hirst, 'Liberal Education and the Nature of Knowledge', reprinted in P.H. Hirst, *Knowledge and the Curriculum*, London, Routledge & Kegan Paul, 1974.
18 L.A. Reid, *Ways of Knowledge and Experience*, London, Allen & Unwin, 1961.
19 P.H. Hirst, 'What is Teaching?', in R.S. Peters (ed.), *The Philosophy of Education*, London, Oxford University Press, 1973.
20 D.J. O'Connor, 'The Nature of Educational Theory', *Proc. Phil. of Ed. Soc. of G.B.*, Jan. 1972.
21 P.H. Hirst, 'Philosophy and Educational Theory', *British Journal of Educational Studies*, Nov. 1963. See also his papers 'Educational

Theory', in J.W. Tibble (ed.), *The Study of Education*, London, Routledge & Kegan Paul, 1966.

22　R.F. Dearden, 'Theory and Practice in Education', an inaugural lecture at the University of Birmingham, February 1979, reprinted in *Journal of Philosophy of Education*, vol. 14, no. 1, 1980.

23　See also R.S. Peters, 'Motivation in Education', in *Essays on Educators*, London, Allen & Unwin, 1981.

24　R.S. Peters (ed.), *Perspectives on Plowden*, op. cit.

25　R.S. Peters (ed.), *The Role of the Head*, London, Routledge & Kegan Paul, 1976.

26　S.C. Brown and J.P. White, 'Learning', *Proc. Aristotelian Soc.*, supp. vol. 1972. See also F. Dunlop, 'Human Nature, Learning and Ideology', *Brit. Journ. Ed. Studies*, Oct. 1977, and G.M. Langford, 'Learning and Knowledge', *Journ. of Phil. of Ed.*, 1978.

27　D.W. Hamlyn, 'Human Learning, The Logical and Psychological Aspects of Learning', in R.S. Peters (ed.), *The Philosophy of Education*, London, Oxford University Press, 1973, and *Experience and the Growth of Understanding*, London, Routledge & Kegan Paul, 1978. R.S. Peters (ed.), *The Concept of Education*, London, Routledge & Kegan Paul, 1967, brings together a collection of useful articles on processes of education.

28　R.M. Hare, 'Language and Moral Education', in G. Langford and D.J. O'Connor, *New Essays in the Philosophy of Education*, London, Routledge & Kegan Paul, 1973, and F. Dunlop, 'Form, Content and Rationality in Moral Education', *Proc. Phil. of Ed. Soc. of G.B.*, July 1977.

29　R.S. Peters, *Psychology and Ethical Development*, London, Allen & Unwin, 1974, chs 11, 15, 16, 17 and 'The Place of Kohlberg's Theory in Moral Education', *Journal of Moral Education*, May 1978.

30　M.F.D. Young (ed.), *Knowledge and Control*, London, Collier-Macmillan, 1971.

31　R. Pring, 'Knowledge out of Control', *Education for Teaching*, Nov. 1972.

32　M.F.D. Young and J.P. White, 'The Sociology of Knowledge', *Education for Teaching*, Autumn 1975 and Spring 1976.

33　A. Flew, *Sociology, Equality and Education*, London, Macmillan, 1976, ch. 2.

34　M. Warnock, *Schools of Thought*, London, Faber & Faber, 1977, ch. 3.

35　R.S. Downie, E. Loudfoot and E. Telfer, *Education and Personal Relationships*, London, Methuen, 1974.

36　G. Langford in G. Langford and D.J. O'Connor, op. cit., ch. 1.

37 M. Warnock, op. cit., p. 12.
38 A. Hartnett and M. Naish, *Theory and the Practice of Education,* London, Heinemann, 1976, vol. 1.
39 W.B. Gallie, 'Essentially Contested Concepts', *Proc. Arist. Soc.,* 1955-6.
40 M. Warnock, op. cit., ch. 4.
41 R.M. Hare, op. cit.
42 R.K. Elliott, 'Versions of Creativity', *Proc. Phil. of Ed. Soc. of G.B.,* July 1971.
43 J.P. White, 'The Aims of Education: three legacies of the British Idealists', *Journal of Phil. of Ed.,* 1978.
44 H.S. Freeman, 'The Concept of Teaching', *Proc. Phil. of Ed. Soc. of G.B.,* Jan. 1973.
45 Schools Council/Nuffield Foundation, *The Humanities Project: An Introduction,* London, Heinemann, 1970.
46 C. Bailey, 'Teaching by Discussion and the Neutral Teacher', and J. Elliott, 'Neutrality, Rationality and the Role of the Teacher', *Proc. Phil. of Ed. Soc. of G.B.,* Jan. 1973.
47 M. Warnock and R. Norman, 'The Neutral Teacher', in S.C. Brown, op. cit.
48 R.M. Hare and P.D. Walsh, 'Value Education in a Pluralist Society', *Proc. Phil. of Ed. Soc. of G.B.,* Jan. 1973.
49 See J. Wilson, 'Education and Indoctrination', and R.M. Hare, 'Adolescents into Adults', in T.H.B. Hollins (ed.), *Aims in Education: the Philosophic Approach,* Manchester University Press, 1964; I. Snook, *The Concept of Indoctrination,* London, Routledge & Kegan Paul, 1970; J.P. White, 'Indoctrination', in R.S. Peters (ed.), *The Concept of Education,* London, Routledge & Kegan Paul, 1967; I.M. Gregory and R.G. Woods, 'Indoctrination', *Proc. Phil. of Ed. Soc. of G.B.,* Jan. 1970; D. Cooper, 'Intentions and Indoctrination', *Educational Philosophy and Theory,* March 1973; I. Snook, *Concepts of Indoctrination,* London, Routledge & Kegan Paul, 1972.
50 W.H. Burston, *Principles of History Teaching,* London, Methuen, 1963; and W.H. Burston and D. Thompson (eds), *Studies in the Nature and Teaching of History,* London, Routledge & Kegan Paul, 1967.
51 C.P. Ormell and M. Elliott, 'Ideology and the Reform of School Mathematics', *Proc. Phil. of Ed. Soc. of G.B.,* Jan. 1969.
52 P. Stevens, 'On the Nuffield Philosophy of Science', *Journal of Philosophy of Education,* July 1978.
53 R. Carlisle and M. Adams, 'The Concept of Physical Education', *Proc. Phil. of Ed. Soc. of G.B.,* July 1975.

54 D. Aspin, 'Ethical Aspects of Sports and Games in Physical Education', *Proc. Phil. of Ed. Soc. of G.B.*, July 1975.

55 D. Carr, 'Practical Pursuits and the Curriculum', *Journal of Philosophy of Education*, July 1978.

56 R.F. Dearden, 'Competition in Education', *Proc. Phil. of Ed. Soc. of G.B.*, Jan. 1972; M. Fielding, 'Against Competition', *Proc. Phil. of Ed. Soc. of G.B.*, July 1976. See also L.R. Perry, 'Competition and Co-operation', *Brit. Journ. Ed. Studies*, June 1975.

57 W.H. Hudson, 'Is Religious Education Possible?', in G. Langford and D. J. O'Connor, op. cit.

58 R. Marples and R. Attfield, 'Is Religious Education Possible?', in *Journal of Philosophy of Education*, July 1978.

59 See, for example, E. Cox, *Changing Aims in Religious Education*, London, Routledge & Kegan Paul, 1966.

60 P.H. Hirst, 'Morals, Religion and the Maintained School', in P.H. Hirst, *Knowledge and the Curriculum*, London, Routledge & Kegan Paul, 1974.

61 P. McPhail, J.R. Ungoed-Thomas and H. Chapman, *Moral Education in the Secondary School*, London, Longman, 1972.

62 M. Warnock, op. cit.

63 J.P. White, *Towards a Compulsory Curriculum*, London, Routledge & Kegan Paul, 1973.

64 R.F. Dearden, *The Philosophy of Primary Education*, op. cit.

65 R. Pring, *Knowledge and Schooling*, London, Open Books, 1976; 'Common Sense and Education', *Proc. Phil. of Ed. Soc. of G.B.*, July 1977; and 'Curriculum Integration', in R.S. Peters (ed.), *The Philosophy of Education*, London, Oxford University Press, 1973.

66 P.H. Hirst, 'Curriculum Integration', in *Knowledge and the Curriculum*, London, Routledge & Kegan Paul, 1974.

67 H. Sockett, *Designing the Curriculum*, London, Open Books, 1976, and 'Curriculum Planning: Taking a Means to an End', in R.S. Peters (ed.), *The Philosophy of Education*, London, Oxford University Press, 1973.

68 R. Barrow, *Common-sense and the Curriculum*, London, Allen & Unwin, 1976.

69 S.C. Brown and A.P. Griffiths, 'Academic Freedom', in S.C. Brown (ed.), op. cit.

70 D.E. Cooper and T. O'Hagan, 'Quality and Equality in Education', in S.C. Brown (ed.), op. cit.

71 M. Warnock, op. cit., chs 1, 2.

72 See J. Rawls, op. cit.

73 J. Wilson, *Philosophy and Practical Education*, London, Routledge & Kegan Paul, 1977, ch. 3.

74 P.S. Wilson, *Interest and Discipline in Education*, London, Routledge & Kegan Paul, 1971. See also P. Moore and P.S. Wilson, 'Perspectives on Punishment', *Proc. Phil. of Ed. Soc. of G.B.*, Jan. 1974.

75 See D. Bridges, *Education, Democracy & Discussion*, Windsor, NFER, 1979; and D. Bridges and P. Scrimshaw, *Values and Authority in Schools*, London, Hodder & Stoughton, 1975; D. Bridges, 'What's the use of Meetings?', *Proc. Phil. of Ed. Soc. of G.B.*, July 1975; and P.H. Hirst and R.S. Peters, *The Logic of Education*, London, Routledge & Kegan Paul, 1970, ch. 7.

76 I.M. Gregory, 'The Right to Education', and C. Wringe, 'Pupils' Rights', *Proc. Phil. of Ed. Soc. of G.B.*, Jan. 1973.

77 See, for instance, G. Haydon, 'The "Right to Education" and Compulsory Schooling', *Educational Philosophy and Theory*, March 1977.

78 P.A. White, 'Education, Democracy and the Public Interest', in R.S. Peters (ed.), *The Philosophy of Education*, London, Oxford University Press, 1973.

79 P.A. White, 'Work-place Democracy and Political Education', *Journal of Philosophy of Education*, July 1979.

80 H. Sockett, 'Teacher Accountability', *Proc. Phil. of Ed. Soc. of G.B.*, July 1976.

81 J.P. White, 'Teacher Accountability and School Autonomy', *Proc. Phil. of Ed. Soc. of G.B.*, July 1976.

82 M. Warnock, op. cit., ch. 4.

83 D.W. Hamlyn, *Experience and the Growth of Understanding*, London, Routledge & Kegan Paul, 1978.

84 R. Barrow, *Plato, Utilitarianism and Education*, London, Routledge & Kegan Paul, 1975.

85 See R.K. Elliott, 'Versions of Creativity', *Proc. Phil. of Ed. Soc. of G.B.*, July 1971; 'Education, Love of one's Subject and Love of Truth', *Proc. Phil. of Ed. Soc. of G.B.*, Jan. 1974; 'The Concept of Development', *Proc. Phil. of Ed. Soc. of G.B.*, Jan. 1975; 'Education and Justification', *Proc. Phil. of Ed. Soc. of G.B.*, Jan. 1977; 'Education and Human Being', in S.C. Brown (ed.), op. cit.

86 J. Wilson, *Education in Religion and the Emotions*, London, Heinemann, 1971.

87 R.S. Peters, 'The Education of the Emotions', in R.S. Peters, *Psychology and Ethical Development*, London, Allen & Unwin, 1974.

88 J.-J. Rousseau, *Emile*, London, Everyman eds, 1911, p. 10.

89 W. Golding, *The Lord of the Flies*, London, Faber & Faber, 1954.

90 R.S. Peters, 'Dilemmas in Liberal Education', in R.S. Peters, *Educa-*

tion and the Education of Teachers, London, Routledge & Kegan Paul, 1977.

91   R. Barrow, *Radical Education*, London, Martin Robertson, 1978.

92   R. Dearden, *Problems of Primary Education*, op. cit.

93   See R. Dearden, 'The Assessment of Learning', *Brit. Journ. Ed. Studies*, June 1979.

3 The history of education

Brian Simon

I

It is just over a hundred years since R.H. Quick published his pioneering book, *Essays on Educational Reformers* (1868), a volume written with all the passion of youth, and in many ways the model for much of the first wave of writing in the history of education in this country. Essentially this summarised and provided a civilised discussion of the ideas of certain great educators of the past, though Quick used the opportunity to launch a polemic against what he saw as the arid, verbalising tendency of the Renaissance educators, responsible, he thought, for contemporary discontents; and for popularising the approach of Pestalozzi, Froebel and Spencer of whose stance, generally speaking, he clearly approved. This was history with a message.

Around the turn of the century, several contributions were made to the history of ideas in education, which now constituted the central approach; for instance, by Oscar Browning, S.S. Laurie, W.H. Woodward and others.[1] It was Quick's view that, by systematically studying the 'great thinkers', it was possible to penetrate into the science of education and winnow out its principles. 'By considering the great thinkers in chronological order,' he wrote, 'we see what each adds to the treasure which he finds already accumulated, and thus by degrees we are arriving in education, as in most departments of human endeavour, at a *science*. In this science lies our hope for the future.'[2]

Such an approach is today at a discount. Quick, who would hardly have claimed to be a historian, presented the ideas of his 'great thinkers, out of context, as worthy of study in themselves – for their intrinsic value. This approach, which forms one strand in the history of education, was paralleled in the late nineteenth and early twentieth centuries by quite a different genus, having different interests and objectives and using an entirely different set of data, best described as institutional history. The main proponent of this approach, A.F. Leach, an assistant charity commissioner, was professionally concerned with seeking out and determining the origin, status and ownership of endowed institutions in particular. If modern scholarship no longer accepts Leach's main conclusion, as to the supposed disastrous effect of the Reformation on English schooling, nevertheless the branch of historical scholarship Leach pioneered is still with us and has made its contribution to our understanding. But the entire separation of institutional from what might be called ideological historical studies hardly contributed to the interpretation of the relations between ideological and institutional change, nor of the relation of either or both these to social change generally. Nor was the situation necessarily improved with what may be called the third genus of historical studies in the field of education: the narrative study of educational systems, or parts of systems, with the focus on parliamentary acts, and the great men, or politicians, held responsible – as in the Forster Act, the Balfour Act, the Fisher Act, the Butler Act and the like.

It would, of course, be ridiculous, and unhistorical, to denigrate, or underestimate, what educational historians achieved in the period covered by these writers – roughly 70 to 80 years since Quick's first book was published. In the early years of this century much was produced, some of it undoubtedly of lasting value. Reference may be made in

63

particular to the work of Foster Watson, of J.W. Adamson, who held one of the first named Chairs in the history of education at King's College, London, and of many others. Among these should be included the social historians J.L. and Barbara Hammond who first drew attention to crucial aspects of popular education, A.E. Dobbs of King's College, Cambridge, whose *Education and Social Movements*, published in 1919, was certainly a pioneering work, particularly as concerns the involvement of the early labour movement, and, of course, the great French historian Elie Halévy – the one general historian of either country who really understood and appreciated the importance of education in its relation to social and political development, devoting much attention to it in his brilliant set of volumes on the history of England. The present generation of historians of education has inherited a fruitful corpus of work, despite the divisions and weaknesses referred to earlier.

II

There has been an explosion of work in this field over the last twenty years or so and Quick, I am sure, would be glad to know that a History of Education Society was in fact established some ten years ago, and, indeed, that an international (or all-European) society was brought into being in 1979; that in the United States, in Australia, New Zealand, in Scotland, Japan, and several European countries including West Germany, flourishing societies exist, with their publication outlets, journals, newsletters, and so on. The British society, with over 400 members, is by now well established, and, of course, approaches and ideologies among its membership differ. Each of the approaches of the past still has its acolytes, even if most historians now recognise the need to relate interpretations of educational developments in the past to their wider economic, social and political context. In this paper I am specifically explicating my own approach to the study of history of education.

To deal first with a question which perhaps lies at the root of all others – why study the history of education at all? After all, it's all dead, gone, finished – what is important lies in the future. Maybe it's useful to know something about history in general, but if historians are criticised for ignoring education, well, weren't they right? The history of education is boring, arid, defunct. Such as it is, it were better forgotten.

And what is the answer to that challenge? Certainly the psychologist can teach us about the nature of the child, critical stages in maturation, can throw light on processes of learning and even perhaps of teaching; sociologists can contribute relevant knowledge about the school and class as dynamic organisations, analyse differential opportunities by social class, and, if of the breed of the 'new sociology', attempt to explicate how individual children construct their world and how it is that certain forms of 'what counts as knowledge' are 'made available' to some and not to others. The philosophers can help us to clarify our educational discourse conceptually. But who is to explicate what actually exists in the here and now? Who is to answer the question *why* we have these particular structures, arrangements, procedures, processes and no other? Who is to penetrate into the social and ideological movements of the past of which the present is the expression? Without such an awareness, I suggest, we are rudderless. The drive to historical investigation is the drive to understanding. Not all need such an understanding, but I suggest that all those professionally engaged in education do.

Is this an overstatement – too evangelical? I think not. It is this desire to seek origins, to grasp processes, to assess tendencies, to isolate, identify and cast light on the dynamics of educational change which has motivated historians in the past as well as today. At the start of study in this field, Foster Watson, a student from Tout's famous school of historians at Manchester University, put it like this: it was, he said, the development of science that 'increasingly pressed upon the notice of students the importance of the genetic method of treatment of subjects ... From the very development of scientific conceptions there arose the new scientific demand for the study of the historical side of humanistic subjects', adding that 'it is realised in the outer world of nature that the slightest attempts to analyse the present state of an organism leads us to the past – for what is the past but the antecedent states of the parts which in their organised form now constitute the present'.[3] To understand the present we must study the past.

So much, I think, might find general acceptance, but the issue then arises – what is the scope of such a study and how is this to be defined?

What we are concerned with, I suggest, are the main formative influences on new generations in particular – but sometimes on the older as well. Historians of education have tended, traditionally, to confine their attention to institutionalised education, to schools, universities and the like, and this is understandable as a start. But two points may be made here: firstly that, historically, institutionalised education as such has affected only a minority – and until recently a very small minority – of populations, so that such a concentration or focus involves the exclusion of the mass of mankind (and this is still the case in large areas of the world); and secondly, even with the rise of universal education in advanced industrial countries, crucially important formative influences are left out of account.

Perhaps I can say a word about each of these. It has been a main and telling criticism, over the last twenty years, of American educational history that its focus was confined to the history of the public system of education – in particular to the rise of the common school in the United States. In his seminal work of 1960, *Education in the Forming of American Society*, Bernard Bailyn specifically made this his main point of attack. Historians of education, content with this approach, and concerned primarily to enthuse prospective teachers with a concept of the consistently progressive nature of education in the United States, its civilising and harmonising function, made no attempt at an overall reconstruction of formative educational influences operating in society as a whole, for instance in the seventeenth and eighteenth centuries. Instead they picked on those developments which presaged the later great expansion of institutionalised education; developments which, at that time, were infinitesimal, affecting very few in scattered areas. The result was a complete distortion of the historical record with its concomitant, a serious failure of understanding. The changing role of the family in upbringing, of the local community, of apprenticeship, in particular of the churches and of parish organisation and activities – all these, and much more, were left entirely out of account in favour of a rosy-hued picture of the consistent and apparently inevitable growth of the system of public institutionalised education. According to Bailyn, education should be seen as the whole process of acculturation; the historian of education must necessarily take the whole social context (of which institutionalised education formed only a small part) into account, if he wishes to unravel things as they really were – and to seek explanations of the directions of development.

While Bailyn's equation of education with acculturation perhaps carries things too far – since it is difficult to see what is specific to the history of education in this formulation – there is no doubt whatever that his foray into this field of study has been highly productive, sparking an intense discussion in the United States in particular as to the definition of the field, and promoting a much wider view than that which dominated such studies in the past. This is not the place to go into the passionate debates, the work of the revisionists, as they are called, headed by Michael Katz and others, the subsequent criticisms of the counter-revisionists, and all the others.[4] This phenomenon reflects the continual conditions of crisis that seem to have affected education in the United

States since the late 1950s, and much of this, concerning methodology and approach, raising ideological and directly political issues, is the result not so much of Bailyn's original critique, as of the conflict, heart-searchings, and above all the disenchantment with education as a panacea which has, historically, been such a feature of the American people's approach and evaluation of education.

My second point is that, even with the rise of institution-alised education – the provision of mass universal schooling – the focus on this alone leaves crucially important formative influences out of account. There are, I suggest, two main classes of such influences, at least in advanced industrial countries. First, there are the mass media – the press (especially the mass circulation newspapers) and TV, a comparatively recent phenomenon. I think Lawrence Cremin (of Teachers' College, Columbia) is right when he draws attention to the importance of both of these, but particularly the latter (though it should be said that the mass circulation newspapers as we have them in this country are unknown in the United States).[5] Urie Bronfenbrenner, in his fascinating *Two Worlds of Childhood* (1970), a comparative study of upbringing in the United States and the USSR, shows the extent of mass TV viewing by the young in the United States today. It averages out at about 22 hours per week or a total, by the age of sixteen, of 15,000 hours (the title, incidentally, of a recent research study based on the time a child of sixteen will have spent in school). What is its content and how does it mould, form, the views and character of the rising generation? The same goes for the press and there are, of course, other agencies to which both young and old are subjected both now and in the past. A classic of this kind, I suggest, in a rather different but similar area, is R.K. Webb's brilliant study entitled *The British Working Class Reader* (1955), focusing on the educative influence of the mass production of radical journals in the half-century to 1850 or so. This opens up the whole area of popular literature, from the first translations of the Bible through the pamphlet literature which proliferated in the seventeenth century and even earlier, to the specific production of children's literature from the early nineteenth century to today. Much of this is relatively unexplored territory, but may prove to conceal goldmines. How, for instance, do we assess the great children's journals which took quite a new form in the 1860s, with the production of *Aunt Judy's, Sunshine* and the rest, beamed as they were, to the children of the new nuclear middle-class families; encapsulating, and attempting to perpetuate, the dominant values of that class at that particular time?

But there is also a third point, though this bears some relation to the first – and that is the educative influence of powerful social movements. This was, of course, a central issue in Dobbs's book of 60 years ago. To take one example; one has only to look through the biographies – or better autobiographies – of the leaders of the democratic, popular movements of the early nineteenth century to begin to form an understanding as to how far actual participation in such broadly based movements, in these cases for the regeneration of society, was an actual formative experience for those who participated; how their consciousness was formed, as Marx would have put it, through their activity. The classics here are Samuel Bamford's *Passages in The Life of a Radical*, focusing on the struggle for bread and the vote culminating in Peterloo, and of a later vintage, the Chartist leader's *Life and Struggles of William Lovett in his pursuit of Bread, Knowledge and Freedom* (as he titled it). But there are many others: *The Life of Thomas Cooper* by himself; Holyoake's *Sixty Years of an Agitator's Life*, and so on. The early socialist, or Owenite movement, was highly educative to its participants, as was the still earlier movement of the democratic societies of the 1790s – the Society for Constitutional Information and the Corresponding Societies which flourished in the provincial cities as well as London. Professor Goodwin's fascinating recent book on this subject. *The Friends of Liberty*, specifically stresses the educative implications of this broad, democratic movement which succeeded at its height in

69

invoking mass involvement in its activities. Indeed, although some periods were more dramatic than others, in each the struggles, leading to new forms of organisation, the attempt to win adherents, ideological activity together with direct social and political activity, have been educative in the deepest sense. All these experiences, perpetuated in the memories, attitudes and customs of the people, if only through family tradition, have formed part of the warp and woof of contemporary society. They have determined attitudes, relationships, institutionalised in various ways, in the press, in actual education institutions, in political and social standpoints.

None of these can be ignored by the historian of education, seeking to unravel the tendencies and conflicts forming contemporary society. And, since I have chosen radical social movements as my examples, we cannot ignore the educative influences of those social organisations formed to counter these influences, to stabilise the existing order of things as it was at any given moment in time. Keeping to the nineteenth century, I have in mind the church and its peripheral organisations such as the YMCA and YWCA, the Settlement Movement of the 1880s, the Boys' Brigade and the Scouts, the Girls' Friendly Societies and the like, even the Primrose League – all products of the 1880s or thereabouts. If youth was open not only to corruption and the supposed demoralising tendencies of the Penny Dreadfuls, were they not also to be shielded from the potentially subversive doctrines propagated with immense zeal, energy and apparent success by the revival of socialism at that time – a movement best documented in Edward Thompson's classic life of William Morris, published now a full generation ago? All this brings to mind the concept of the organisation and structure of civil society, as conceived by Gramsci, as the defence in depth of existing social relations in the conditions of advanced industrial society. But perhaps this opens up too wide a field to enter here.

Having said all this, I suppose I must accept that it is the field of organised, institutionalised education that must form the core of our studies, though I would rapidly enter the caveat at the start that, to obtain any real understanding, this must be seen and interpreted in its social, political and often religious context. For it can be argued that institutionalised education, more especially of the mass universal variety, has been a *response* to the indigenous efforts of the people to educate themselves, in their own way, according to their own objectives and aspirations, rather than a function, as it were, benevolently conferred on the masses from above with purely philanthropic ends in view. And that the form mass education has taken, and still takes, has been largely conditioned by this aspect of its origin and development. This is to leave aside, of course, such influences as the effect of urbanisation in the practical, material sense, and of the decline of religious beliefs and forms in the ideological sense. But can the astonishing success of the Sunday School movement in the 1790s and, later, of the Monitorial Schools in the second decade of the nineteenth century or of the Mechanics' Institutes in the third, not be closely related to the developing consciousness of the working class of itself as a class; its widespread efforts to seek understanding and knowledge, its development, under the harshest conditions, of indigenous educational forms, its creation and support for a press reflecting its outlook, all of which presented, or were perceived as presenting, a potential threat to the social order culminating in Chartism? There are those who interpret the imposition of universal compulsory education in the 1870s and 1880s as a deliberate act designed to nullify, lay waste, and destroy indigenous, and above all, independent educational forms. Such an interpretation seems, however, simplistic, since that decision appears as a resultant of a highly complex set of circumstances, of disparate objectives among different social groups or classes. However that may be, at least the example serves to underline my point, which is that the evolution of educational systems, their changing character and procedures, cannot be understood if considered and analysed as things in themselves – even if such systems also

71

have their own inner development which can and must be analysed historically; that inner development is continuously conditioned by external circumstances, as surely we see very clearly today.

It is now a commonplace that institutionalised education tends to reflect class structure. After all, nearly 50 years have passed since R.H. Tawney, in his inaugural lecture as Professor of Economic History at the London School of Economics, said that Marx opened 'a new chapter in historical discussion, which two generations after his death, is still unclosed'. If we substitute four generations now for Tawney's two, we can see that the door is wider open than ever, since new varieties of Marxism sprout every day. So it certainly remains true, as Tawney went on to put it, that, Insofar as it is concerned with the economic foundations of society (which, of course, underlie class functions and relations), serious history today, whether Marxism or not, is inevitably post-Marxian'.[6]

As one who originally assimilated his Marxism, such as it is, as a stimulating aspect of the sub-culture – or better, counter-culture – of the student world at Cambridge in the 1930s, it was, I suppose, inevitable that, when I first turned to the history of education I tended to seek an interpretation in terms of the changing relations of different social classes in the period in which I was interested – at that time from the late eighteenth to the late nineteenth centuries. It seemed to me then, as it still does today, that Marx's model made sense of the turbulent, and often seemingly chaotic events of that hundred years – more especially if account is taken of the shifting relations between social classes consequent upon changing forms of production and exchange and, particularly, of the dynamics of the inner development of systems of education brought into being, or reinforced, to serve the interests of these classes; interests sometimes allied, sometimes opposed. Further, this approach, as I understood it, illuminated the relationship not only of structural change to social change generally, but of both of these to ideological change. It provided the key, therefore, to making sense of the movement of ideas in education, concerning the content of education as well as methodology and procedures – and of the conflicts within these spheres. Finally, as indicated earlier, it enabled penetration into the relationship between changes in the educational system or systems, and social, religious, economic and political movements in society generally.

This sort of interpretation was rendered easier by the fact that, the more one got into the subject, the more evident it became that the Victorians themselves saw education at least partially in this light. In reforming or recasting the system, as they set out to do in mid-century, they tackled the question overtly as a class issue, and, perhaps since these were before the days of compulsory education and political democracy as we know it today, made no bones whatever about it in their published statements. Here my favourite quotation is that by Lord Harrowby in his evidence to the Schools Inquiry Commission, of which he was also a member, a quotation repeated in the report of the Commission. 'I should like to club the grammar schools with some relation to locality, and I should like to say, you shall be a lower middle class school; you shall be a middle middle class school; and you shall be a higher middle class school, that which is now called a grammar school.'[7] And this, of course, the Commission recommended. So we have the definition of three levels among the middle class, with whose education the Schools Inquiry Commission was specifically concerned. Outside there was the new system of so-called public schools for the gentry, aristocracy, and wealthier middle class and the professional groups related to these classes (the clergy, the military, and so on), and below them all, the schools with which the Newcastle Commission was concerned, for the labouring poor, the working classes, or the masses. Within both the systems organised for these two latter classes there were subtle distinctions. As John Hurt has shown in his book,[8] the working class is perhaps better defined as the working classes, and specific distinctions reflecting these sub-groupings developed within the elementary school system, while the subtle (or not so subtle) social

73

distinctions within the new system of public schools has so far defied analysis (a fascinating beginning has been made here by the work of John Honey).[9] In each of these types of schools, I would argue, what might be called 'appropriate' pedagogical means were elaborated, explicable in terms of their social function. In the crudest terms, there were obvious differences between the pedagogy, or total system of upbringing, as practised at Eton, and that practised in the elementary schools in the steel-making area of Sheffield, as described by Cheryl Parsons in her book.[10] More subtle distinctions will be found across the whole spectrum.

It might seem that this interpretation is in danger of offering an over-mechanistic, simplistic interpretation of the relations between education and society, in which the provision of education is seen as the simple *reflection* of existing class relations, or occupational structure. Some historians, who certainly cannot be accused of this form of reductionism, have themselves seen it that way. Thus Geoffrey Best characterises mid-Victorian education as not only reflecting class differences, but as deliberately erected to perpetuate them, and, of course, in the eyes of the chief architects of the system, this was probably the case. Educational systems, he writes, 'can hardly help mirroring the ideas about social relationships of the societies that produce them'. Education became a 'trump card' in the great class competition. The result was that the schools of Britain not only mirrored the hierarchical social structure, 'but were made more and more to magnify its structure in detail'.[11]

But such an interpretation, if applied generally and in a mechanistic form, leaves a great deal out of account and cannot, in itself, offer any interpretation of change. Careful study of the history of education indicates that the issue is far more complex than is dreamt of in this philosophy. The *intentions* of particular social classes or of groups, strata or even individuals, are seldom realised in the pure form desired. It is commonly agreed, for instance, that the early Sunday Schools, however they may have been intended to form the labouring poor to the virtues of obedience, conformity and Christian resignation, in fact, given the circumstances of the time, produced many working men, in the words of Samuel Bamford, 'of sufficient talent to become readers, writers and speakers in the village meetings for parliamentary reform'.[12] So also the historian of Manchester noted in 1851 how the Sunday School teachers 'with the single undeviating purpose of promoting the eternal welfare of their pupils', were in fact 'preparing them for the fit discharge of their social and public duties. They were creating *thought* among the hitherto unthinking masses.'[13]

As things worked out, the form evolved for preparing children with one very specific aim in view was taken over by the democratic movement for quite opposite purposes. The Sunday Schools organised in connection with the Hampden Clubs or the Political Protestants of the north of England, which included adults as well as children, were organs of political education and activity, having as their aim radical social change.[14]

So educational movements may be and have been transformed according to the purposes of those they comprehend, a truth of which the adherents of the concept of education as primarily a means of social control (as it is called) need to be aware. On a different level, and at a different time, the same is true of the dramatic upthrust of elementary education under the advanced school boards in the 1890s, 'citadels of radicalism', as Halévy defined them, when the perspective of creating organic, cohesive, local systems of education under democratic control, covering the whole range from elementary school to university, quite suddenly seemed to become a realisable and to some a horrifying perspective. This movement was the result of pupils, parents, teachers and school board members together consciously developing the system, only established some twenty years earlier, through the setting up of the so-called higher grade schools, local support for technical institutions, colleges and even universities. So the system set up with quite limited, specifically defined objectives was being transformed; was on the edge, it could be argued, of quite decisive developments. This needs to be recognised by anyone seeking an interpretation of the series of drastic – even Draconian – legal, administrative and finally legislative measures carried through by a Conservative government in the period 1899 to 1904; including the actual abolition of the offending school boards (accused of 'extravagance'), the establishment of a secondary system apart, and quite separate from, the elementary system, and the confining of the latter once again, though now even more firmly, within rigid, strictly defined limits.[15] Some may see a parallel in this today.

So we need to bring what the Marxist calls dialectics into play. Systems of education, like other phenomena, need to be seen in terms of their growth, development and decay, of the inner contradictions to which they are subject, and of their interconnections with political, social and economic phenomena. Interpretations of the development of education, of its social role, which ignore its complex, dynamic character, not only present a distorted picture, but also run the danger of being a-historical in their approach – but of this, more later.

III

And what of the relation between structure and ideology, or, if you like, the theory of education? How do we fit this into our schema? Or are such theories the products of minds uncontaminated by any contact with a particular society, or with any specific social class within that society? Are they, in fact, the simple resultant of the progress of mind as Quick, for instance, seemed to believe?

It is enough, perhaps, to pose the problem in that way nowadays to indicate that such an interpretation is untenable. In education, as in other areas where theoretical issues arise, there is a relation of some sort between ideas, the dominant ideology (or ideologies) of the time, and what Marxists call 'the base' – that is, the mode of production and the social relations arising therefrom. The problem is to tease this out, because such relationships are complex; there is nothing simple or 'obvious' about them – particularly in areas like education, far removed from production.

In discussing this I want to focus on one example, albeit a crucial one for educational theory and practice; and that is ideas about human educability which directly affect the teacher and teaching, and indeed the structuring of systems. This has contemporary significance not only because controversy on this issue is still with us, but more particularly because we are only just emerging from a period lasting some 40 to 50 years when one specific set of ideas achieved what may accurately be referred to as hegemonic status over the whole field of education. I refer to psychometry, more particularly the field of mental testing, and the set of ideas as we now realise built into the technology developed to support the theories at the start, the chief of which was the absolute primacy of heredity in the determination of human intellectual capacity, its fixed and unchanging character, the ineffectiveness of education or of the child's life experiences to bring about any change in this inborn power or quality, and the possibility of measuring this quality accurately by means of tests.

It is difficult now to reconstruct the extent to which these doctrines held sway in the recent past. To quote from an historical study published in 1981:

In the 1920's the psychometric intelligence theory achieved hegemony within a mere decade, and received a fulsome accolade of approval in the Hadow Report (1931) and later in an even more decisive form in the Spens Report (1938), which formed the main basis of the Education Act of 1944. Its rise to hegemony was easy, swift and almost total: psychometric theory became the new orthodoxy at all significant levels – at the Board of Education, among

77

local education authorities in official reports and other government publications on education, in educational theory, in teacher training manuals and, if only because of the use of group intelligence tests for secondary school selection, in schools. In short, within the space of a few years it achieved an iron grip on educational theory and practice which was still not undermined in any significant way until the early 1950's and has still not been completely broken.[16]

No attempt can be made here at a detailed analysis as to why this particular set of ideas achieved this position – here quite accurately set out – at this particular moment in time.[17] The source of the primacy of this outlook needs to be sought not only in the history of ideas (and particularly the influence of Darwinism on the one hand, and of philosophic idealism on the other), but also in the actual circumstances of the time which called insistently for theories which legitimised the hierarchical system of education brought into being from 1902 and now under increasing pressure. No more insistent demand was made on the psychologist, wrote Cyril Burt in 1921, than that for a simple mental footrule; which he and others set out to supply.[18] However that may be, we may note that, until the rise of psychometry in the early years of this century, educational theory generally espoused an opposite idea of the potential of human development, stressing the plasticity of the human mind, or brain, its inherent educability and capacity for change – given always the correct conditions. A study of the textbooks or manuals for student teachers in the 1890s brings out absolutely clearly that these were the theories then espoused and propagated. Indeed in his lectures 100 years ago at Cambridge, J.G. Fitch, speaking about the theory of education, specifically elaborated this approach – based, of course, on the theory of associationism, recently reformulated by Alexander Bain in *Education as a Science* (1879) – whose origins we seek among the philosophers of the Enlightenment, and trace back to the work of David Hartley and John Locke.[19] The theories embodied in mental testing, in fact, meant a complete reversal of a long tradition which stressed as fundamental the formative power of education.

Certainly key issues arise. Why was it, for instance, that theories concerning the primacy of hereditary endowment in the distribution of intelligence, already propagated with considerable force by Francis Galton in 1869 (in *Hereditary Genius*), apparently made no impact whatever on educational thinking or policy before 1900? A thorough search of relevant teacher training manuals, HMI reports, and the like indicate that this was the case.[20] What were the circumstances that allowed these theories, admittedly now brought to a certain pitch of technical perfection by the application of statistical expertise, to carry all before them in the period 1925 or so to 1955 or later? And, to take the matter one step further, what were the reasons why these theories, and their educational application, were then discredited, and by psychologists themselves, to such an extent that their leading practitioner and theorist was led to *inventing* new data of a very specific kind in an attempt to perpetuate their hegemony? Cyril Burt, in fully accepting the assumptions underlying the whole so-called 'science' of mental testing, was, as Hearnshaw states in his recent biography, very much a child of his time. His nefarious deeds in the 1950s and 1960s are, I suggest, more satisfactorily explained in terms of the power of ideology to enter into and blind the scientist, than in terms of his own personal psychological make-up, or his genetic constitution in terms of his Celtic origins, as Hearnshaw suggests.[21]

I have chosen one example, and it is perhaps one of the most striking. There appears to be a clear relationship between the economic and social conditions obtaining in the inter-war period, one of stagnation, economic depression, and mass unemployment, the structured, hierarchic system of education then obtaining, and the dominant theory legitimising and lubricating this system or structure, a theory which profoundly affected the approach to teaching and school and classroom practice. This is the period when streaming from the age of seven and below, selection at eleven for different types of school, and the development of differentiated curricula and teaching methods took hold – even the early comprehensive schools erected in the 1950s and later were constructed and planned according to the iron laws of psycho-metry, which dictated their size and their forms of inner organisation both in terms of academic and pastoral functions. It is my contention that similar analyses can and should be made of other periods and systems with the object of teasing out these relationships, so that a fuller understanding of the past which still forms the future, of changes in structure and in pedagogical approaches, may be made.

Educational institutions stand at one remove from the central activity of any society, which is production. Systems and institutions within them have their own inner historical development; practices, procedures and attitudes – the products of earlier historical periods – are tenacious and persist sometimes through the centuries. Current practice is an amalgam – a series, perhaps, of modifications of the past. Much that is 'taken for granted' requires historical investigation if our object is to heighten awareness or consciousness of the real meaning and implications of what exists.

I have attempted to express, in a reasonably brief and I hope comprehensible form, a specific approach to the history of education. There are, of course, other approaches with different foci of interest using different methodologies, but I have deliberately not attempted a survey or critique of these. It will be evident, I hope, from my analysis, that I do not believe, with the French Marxist Althusser, that the complex, dynamic processes of education, an area where the sometimes opposite objectives of different social classes meet and where a struggle reflecting these is constantly being joined – that these complex processes can be subsumed under the concept of an 'Ideological State Apparatus', with the implication that the ideology so propagated is and must be that of the ruling class, and all-powerful.[22] This concept seems to me to contain a half-truth, but in essence to be metaphysical, reductionist and mechanist. Above all, in its implicit denial of the role of historical formation it offends one of the chief concerns of Marxism; at least as presented by Karl Marx himself. Other classes also have their objectives and ideologies, which is the reason why education has historically been, and still is, an area of contention, a grasp of which is essential if development is to be understood.

It will be equally obvious, or at least so I hope, that I do not think educational evolution can be interpreted as the simple reflection of the economic or occupational structure; as if there were some direct linear relationship. This thesis, presented by Bowles and Gintis in their well-known book, *Schooling in Capitalist America* (1976), also contains a half-truth but it is equally open to the charge of mechanism, in that it fails to recognise the complex nature of the relationship between education and economic structure; its mediating role, its degree of relative autonomy.

Nevertheless, the work of both of these (and I would include Bourdieu and Passeron's analysis of this question)[23] has stimulated widespread and serious discussion of the key question of the relations between education and society. Historians of education can and should make a central contribution to this understanding.

Notes

1 See, for instance, Oscar Browning, *An Introduction to the Study of Educational Theories*, London, Kegan Paul, 1881; S.S. Laurie, *Studies in the History of Educational Opinion since the Renaissance*, London, C.J. Clay, 1903; W.H. Woodward, *Studies in Education during the Age of the Renaissance*, Cambridge University Press, 1906.

2 R.H. Quick, *Essays on Educational Reformers*, London, Longmans, 1893 edn, p. 505.

3 Foster Watson, 'The Study of the History of Education', *Contemporary Review*, vol. CV, 1914, p. 85.

4 See, for example, Michael B. Katz, *The Irony of Early School Reform*, Harvard University Press, 1968, and *Class, Bureaucracy and Schools*, New York, Praeger, 1971; also Clarence J. Karier, Paul C. Violas and Joel Spring, *Roots of Crisis; American Education in the Twentieth Century*, New York, Rand McNally, 1973. For an overview, Sol Cohen, 'The History of Urban Education in the United States: Historians of Education and their Discontents', in David Reeder (ed.), *Urban Education in the 19th Century*, London, Taylor & Francis, 1977. Diane Ravitch, in *The Revisionists Revised*, New York, Basic, 1977, presents a counter argument.

5 Lawrence A. Cremin, *Public Education*, New York, Basic, 1976, pp. ix-x. Cremin argues that television 'has fundamentally transformed the context in which all schooling proceeds'.

6 J.M. Winter (ed.), *History and Society, Essays by R.H. Tawney*, London, Routledge & Kegan Paul, 1978, p. 51.

7 *Report of the Schools Inquiry Commission*, I, 579.

8 J.S. Hurt, *Elementary Schooling and the Working Classes, 1860-1918*, London, Routledge & Kegan Paul, 1979.

9 J.R. De S. Honey, *Tom Brown's Universe, the Development of Public Schools in the 19th Century*, London, Millington, 1977.

10 Cheryl Parsons, *Education in an Urban Community*, London, Routledge & Kegan Paul, 1978.

11 Geoffrey Best, *Mid-Victorian Britain, 1851-1875*, London, Weidenfeld & Nicolson, 1973 edn, p. 170.

12 Samuel Bamford, *Passages in the Life of a Radical*, ed. Henry Dunckley, London, Unwin, 1893, p. 12.

13 A. Prentice, *Historical Sketches and Personal Recollections of Manchester*, London, Gilpin, 1851, p. 116.

14 Brian Simon, *Studies in the History of Education, 1780-1870*, London, Lawrence & Wishart, 1960, pp. 186-93.

15 Brian Simon, *Education and the Labour Movement, 1870-1920*, London, Lawrence & Wishart, 1965, pp. 165-246.

16 Quoted from J.C.B. Gordon, *Verbal Deficit: a Critique*, 1981.

17 But see Brian Simon, *The Politics of Educational Reform, 1920-1940*, London, Lawrence & Wishart, 1974, pp. 225-50.

18 Cyril Burt, *Mental and Scholastic Tests*, London, P.S. King, 1921, p. 1.

19 J.G. Fitch, *Lectures on Teaching*, 1881, pp. 124ff; David Hartley, *Observations on Man*, 1749; John Locke, *An Essay concerning Human Understanding*, 1693. I am indebted to John Gordon for confirmation of this finding.

20 I am indebted to J.C.B. Gordon for confirmation of this finding.

21 L.S. Hearnshaw, *Cyril Burt, Psychologist*, Cornell University Press, 1979, ch. 13.

22 Louis Althusser, 'Ideology and Ideological State Apparatuses', in *Lenin and Philosophy*, 2nd edn, London, New Left Books, 1977, pp. 123–73.
23 Pierre Bourdieu and Jean Claude Passeron, *Reproduction in Education, Society and Culture*, London, Sage, 1977.

4 Educational psychology

John Nisbet

My subject in this paper is the present state of studies in educational psychology, but to put this in context it is necessary both to look back and to look forward. It would perhaps be a more interesting project to trace the history of educational psychology from its emergence through William James and John Dewey to the momentous basic research of the early Americans on the psychology of the elementary school curriculum, such as Thorndike on the psychology of teaching arithmetic and spelling and Huey on reading. They opened up the rich prairies of this land of educational psychology and reaped great harvests. They were followed by the gleaners, who combed the fields and picked up the occasional straw. After them came the geese who wandered among the stubble, clucking excitedly when they found the odd grain which had been left. By this interpretation of history we are the geese.

But I do not think that this model fits. An alternative portrayal of the past hundred years is of a steadily growing body of science, building up through new theories in the early decades of this century to a peak of achievement in the 1940s and 1950s. Then the heart of educational psychology was the analysis of human abilities, dissected by psychometrics and sophisticated testing. Differentiation of ability was the key to teaching and learning, with diagnostic measures to identify defects and prescribe remedial teaching, with intelligence as the central concept to explain human learning and failures in learning. This mode of explanation has been abandoned progressively since the 1950s, until now, when, if IQ figures at all in courses of training, it is quoted only to illustrate the fallacies of the past. I think this also is a false picture. It reminds me of Gibbon's *Decline and Fall of the Roman Empire*, and it suggests that only the Dark Ages lie ahead for us, with our former stately temples abandoned and in ruins and our gods discredited.

Yet there is some evidence to suggest that educational psychology has been in retreat for the past twenty years and is now a mere shadow of its former self. In the 1940s, psychology dominated education. It was the central science, the source of education's dominant theories. Since then, philosophy and history have re-emerged as major contributors to educational thought; sociology has sprung into importance; economics has had its brief moment; and today the politics of education is the growth point – the analysis of decision-making, policy and control of the curriculum. The vast empire of educational psychology has fragmented, with declarations of UDI by new specialisms. Curriculum development has taken over the psychology of the elementary school curriculum; evaluation and accountability are the new fashionable terms for testing; sociology has annexed human relationships. In all such areas, new experts command the field often without any knowledge of educational psychology except that which they have gained at second hand. In some teacher training courses, psychology has been relegated to the status of an option. I think this view mistaken, that rumours of the death of educational psychology are premature, and that in recent times psychology has made significant advances which offer a promise of a basis for a theory of education, at least in its cognitive aspects. Our successors, looking back over the history of educational psychology, may see the 1970s as a crucial period.

Some years ago, at a conference in London on educational

research and psychology, the editor of the *Times Educational Supplement* attacked educational psychology, and educational research generally, because he claimed there was no consensus – not even any national basis for consensus – in the discipline.[1] I decided therefore for this paper to test whether there was any consensus among psychologists about the present state of educational psychology. I wrote to sixteen of my friends and colleagues, asking 'which are the important and promising developments in educational psychology (and also the topics of declining interest)' but assuring them that I was not asking them to write my paper for me. Five demurred (or didn't reply): one letter produced two replies. Thus I had twelve replies. Four confined their remarks to their own field of study, leaving me a sample of eight.

Of course, this is not an adequate nor a representative sample. However, they were deliberately selected to cover a wide range of interests. In acknowledgment of the long and carefully reasoned replies which they gave me, I would like to name the twelve respondents. In alphabetical order of their university, they were: my colleague Graham Davies from Aberdeen, Ben Morris from Bristol, Paul Kline and Leslie Reid from Exeter, Ann Clarke from Hull, Kenneth Lovell and Margaret Sutherland from Leeds, Derek Wright and Bill Anthony from Leicester, Barbara Tizard from London, Peter Mittler from Manchester and Eric Lunzer from Nottingham. The interpretation of their replies is my own, and does not commit these friends in any way: they are a motley crew, they differed in their priorities, and they raised interesting points which I cannot cover fully here. My first impression on reading the letters was the diversity of their views; but as I worked through the letters there emerged a consensus which I can best express by putting points together in an 'identikit' picture of the present state of educational psychology.

The consensus of opinion is clearest on the unfashionable or unpromising topics, areas of study which were recently considered important but are now seen as offering less promise than formerly. It will come as no surprise to you to learn that psychometrics heads this list.

> I think there is a disenchantment with psychometric assessment, formerly the stock-in-trade of educational psychology.

There is still an 'endless' flow of tests and check-lists, but there has been

> a shift from an interest in the diagnosis and treatment of individuals, to an attempt to alter or study the forces impinging on the individual.

Or, to quote another respondent,

> Psychologists are beginning to move away from their obsessive preoccupation with individual assessment to considering the wide systems in which children live and learn. They are becoming more interested in the social psychology of the school, in staff development and training, and in the way in which children function in families and in social institutions of various kinds.

Or another, more bluntly:

> What is of declining importance? Surely the whole paraphernalia of selection techniques, the statistical attempts to compare methods, etc.

We are not throwing away the achievements of the past fifty years – or at least I hope not. One of the major achievements of educational psychology in the first half of this century has been to establish the importance of individual differences, as a corrective to the methods of mass education which developed in the second half of the nineteenth century. In the nineteenth century, deficiencies in learning were seen as a *moral* lapse, a failure to put enough effort into it, a failure to pay attention and to try. It was to defeat this belief that learning was just a matter of application that Susan Isaacs, in 1932,[2] made her eloquent plea for streaming children into 'fast, medium and slow'; and though we have certainly rejected that over-simple procedure, her basic argument is still valid – that slow learners should not be left behind by teaching directed only at the most able children. Differentiation in terms of ability is still an accepted principle in teaching; and though we require primary school teachers to teach the whole range of ability, it is accepted that this requires flexibility in treating each child as an individual.

However, this model of learning theory, in which success in learning depends on the ability of the learner, on qualities inherent in the 'recipient', is not such a substantial step forward as was thought thirty years ago, when I was a student. The old model saw deficiencies in learning as a moral lapse: the new model sought to explain differences in learning in terms of differences in ability. In order to understand how to teach, you have to study the nature of human abilities. The word 'abilities' appears in the titles of the principal textbooks of the 1940s.[3] The assumption was that if there was a failure in learning, you look for a defect in the learner, something lacking in his ability. But the defect was still seen as located in the learner.

The 1950s and 1960s produced another different model, one which has its origins far back in the early days of psychology – that if there is a failure in learning one should look for defects in the environment of the learner, especially in the early years of childhood, or in the culture or sub-culture, in social disadvantage. I have already quoted the respondent who mentioned the shift of interest from the individual to 'the forces impinging on the individual' – looking for defects in the environment or in social institutions as an explanation of failure to learn.

This explanation of failure was still a moral one, in that it implied a responsibility on society, or on the parents, rather than on the individual – anyone other than the teacher! Both these models, explaining failure in terms of defects in the learner's ability and explaining it in terms of defects in the learner's environment and history, reflect an 'overemphasis on predestination' in developmental psychology (to quote one of my letters). They are explanations which shift the responsibility away from the individuals directly involved in the process, the teacher and learner. It is not the teacher's fault if his pupils are too dull to understand; nor is it the learner's fault if he lacks the neurological equipment to be able to cope, or has been disadvantaged by his social environment, or not talked to sufficiently by his parents!

More recently – though this anticipates my argument – we look for an explanation in the actual teaching he has received, or the context in which the learning has been arranged, a rather obvious point, most teachers would say, surprisingly neglected, and a more challenging diagnosis of failure to learn. Focus on the actual teaching, both content and method, on the social interactions, and on the process of learning, is a more productive way of thinking about it and of explaining success and failure in learning. This is a point which several of my respondents suggested, each in different ways:

a new preoccupation with processes as well as outcomes;

a new interest in process rather than input–output, e.g. classroom observation studies, illuminative evaluation, and in general the study of what is going on in the educational environment.

It is neatly summarised by Entwistle in a *Times Educational Supplement* review of Bruner's *Beyond the Information Given*:

A succession of theorists have suggested limitations on the extent to which teachers can improve the intellectual competence of their pupils. Some . . . have maintained that intelligence is determined genetically to a large extent . . . . Environmentalists have . . . removed this particular shackle, only to replace it by an even tighter one. We

are now besieged by ideas about the disastrous effects of a
poor home background . . . [etc.] [In opposition to these
beliefs] Bruner . . . has consistently preached an optimistic
gospel . . . which emphasises possibilities, not limitations.[4]

The 'optimistic gospel' referred to, unfortunately, can be
interpreted in an over-simple way, to imply that if only we
had enough research and resources for teaching, the right
material, the right method, sufficient time, adequate training
and so on, we could teach everybody everything. Bruner's
brave suggestion was 'the hypothesis that any subject can be
taught effectively in some intellectually honest form to any
child at any stage of development'; but he put it forward as
a hypothesis, not as an article of faith; and its value is that it
directs attention to the subject matter of instruction, its
structure and form, and to the intellectual powers of the
learner, his stage of development and his cognitive frames of
reference, and to the interaction between these, namely the
process of education (which is, in fact, the title of the 1965
book by Bruner from which that quotation was taken[5]).
This is much more complex than the rather wild optimism of
other writers – Maya Pines, for example.[6]

Millions of children are being irreparably damaged by our
failure to stimulate them intellectually during their crucial
years – from birth to five.

– and subsequent chapters in that book are entitled 'Head
Start', 'The New Mind Builders' and 'The Pressure Cooker
Approach'. A more restrained expression of the ideas is to be
found in Medawar's 1959 Reith Lectures, *The Future of
Man*,[7] in which he argues that

We can . . . improve upon nature; but the possibility of our
doing so depends, very obviously, upon our continuing to
explore into nature and to enlarge our knowledge and
understanding of what is going on.

And this, I suggest, is what is happening in educational
psychology – especially in cognitive psychology: by study of

processes of learning and teaching, and of memory and perception and information-processing, we are better able to make progress within the constraints imposed on us, as teachers, by the forces of heredity and environment. Preoccupation with these constraints is a self-inflicted discouragement from experiment and inquiry:

> The bells which toll for mankind are – most of them,
> anyway – like the bells on Alpine cattle; they are attached
> to our own necks, and it must be *our* fault if they do not
> make a cheerful or harmonious sound. (Medawar)[8]

But, to return to my respondents and their consensus on current trends in educational psychology, three themes which several of them mentioned fit the context which I have been trying to describe – first, cognitive psychology and language studies; second, strategies of learning; and third, stages of learning or, more generally, developmental psychology. My aim here is to expound these very briefly, and try to link them in a coherent statement of the relevance of current psychological thinking to education.

For the first of these themes, cognitive psychology, I propose to draw from a paper by Downing, read to the British Psychological Society Education Section in 1975.[9] In that paper he demonstrated very effectively the influence of cognitive psychology on recent educational thinking. Both the 1967 Plowden Report[10] on primary schools and the 1975 Bullock Report[11] on language and the teaching of English, base their recommendations on a cognitive psychological theory which owes a lot to recent work. The psychology is implicit rather than explicit – Bruner gave evidence to the Bullock Committee, but he is not quoted – but occasionally the debt to psychology is openly acknowledged. For example, the Bullock Report mentions 'current theories' without actually specifying whose theories they are, about the role of language in 'generating knowledge and producing new forms of behaviour'.[12] Thus the Bullock Report says:

> We symbolise, or represent to ourselves, the objects,

people and events that make up our environment, and so so cumulatively, thus creating an inner representation of the world as we have encountered it. . . . We interpret what we perceive at any given moment by relating it to our body of past experiences and respond to it in the light of that interpretation.[13]

And specifically on language:

A word that names an object is, for a young child, a filing-pin upon which he stores successive experiences of the objects themselves.[14]

The Bullock Report clearly accepts cognitive theory and rejects behaviourist views, specifically criticising Bereiter and Engelman as 'narrow' and damaging to 'imagination and flexibility', and implicitly when they condemn phonic drill as a method of teaching reading. And in its advocacy of learning by discovery, the Report expresses its case in Bruner terms:

It is a confusion of everyday thought that we tend to regard 'knowledge' as something that exists independently of someone who knows. 'What is known' must, in fact, be brought to life afresh within every 'knower' by his own efforts. To bring knowledge into being is a formulating process. . . . By a kind of spiral, the formulation itself becomes a source from which we draw further questions, fresh hypotheses. . . .[15]

Thus language development increases the child's ability to solve problems.

As often happens, the educational theorists take the psychological theory further than the psychologists themselves might wish. But, to quote one of my respondents, there is

Increasing evidence . . . that the verbal and cognitive processing in the home, and the demands of the sub-culture, make it easier or harder for the individual to use his reasoning powers outside of 'embedded' situations. (Quoting Donaldson and 'a vast literature' in support)[16]

There are plenty of examples from Bruner (particularly *Beyond the Information Given* and *The Relevance of Education*[17]) to match the Bullock quotations:

Man constructs models of his world, not only templates that represent what he encounters . . . but also ones that permit him to go beyond them.[18]

The principle is well summarised by Anglin:

The individual is best viewed neither as a passive recipient of information nor as a bundle of stimulus-response connections. Rather he should be regarded as an active participant in the knowledge-getting process, one who selects and transforms information, who constructs hypotheses and who alters these hypotheses in the face of inconsistent or discrepant evidence.[19]

To do justice to this, I would need to review the work done on memory and information-processing. Those who attended the NATO conference at York in 1980[20] will have heard papers by Hunt and Butterfield and Brown, on related themes: explaining verbal skills in terms of information-processing and memory scanning, explaining handicap in terms of inadequate processing strategies, and using laboratory studies to explain the development of memory skills in children. One of my respondents says:

Cognitive psychology has reached a stage of maturity when its concepts can be usefully applied to educational problems, a view which Broadbent foreshadowed in his 1975 paper in the *British Journal of Educational Psychology.*[21]

The second of my 'consensus themes' is the importance of current work on strategies of learning. Much of this work (particularly that of Pask[22]) derives from information theory, but of course there are many contributions from psychologists like Gagne[23] and from others in education, such as Hudson,[24] who link strategies of learning to personality types. Expressed simply (perhaps crudely), the idea is that there is no one correct method of learning, that each of us develops his or her preferred styles, and that successful learning depends on the structure of the material to be learned as well as on the structures with which the learner approaches the task. There are many clever dichotomies offered to us: Pask's serialists and holists, Hudson's sylbs and sylfs (syllabus-bound and syllabus-free), and Marton's deep-level and surface-level processing.[25] This topic also deserves a paper to itself – I know of at least three people who are currently writing books on this theme – and indeed one of my sample even suggested 'the possibility of it all coming together in a Darwinian revolution of our thinking in educational psychology'. Another, more modestly, wrote:

> Research by R.C. Anderson's group and the many contributors to the ongoing symposium on 'Learning Processes and Strategies' in the *British Journal of Educational Psychology*[26] suggest that psychologists in the field of cognitive learning may at last be able to offer teachers something solid and soundly based which could be of real practical significance. It seems likely that this corpus of material will, in addition, enrich psychological theory.

The third and last of my related themes is the concept of 'stages of development', and this brings in the very influential work of Piaget. There is a measure of agreement that the critical analysis of Piaget's theories, by Bryant and Donaldson, Lovell, Lunzer, and of course Brainerd and others, has corrected the previous over-emphasis on stages and the over-simple interpretation of what they imply for the design of materials and methods of teaching. The idea of 'stages' fits – perhaps too well – with the idea of a variety of strategies of learning and with Bruner's hypothesis quoted earlier that 'any subject can be taught effectively in some intellectually honest form to any child at any stage of development'. But it is too neat in that it may be taken to imply that progress in learning and intellectual development is just a matter of maturation, a point expressed concisely but rather technically by the respondent who wrote:

> An age-related restriction on thinking is confounded by the fact that level of thinking is affected by content, context, meaning of the task for the pupil and his perception of the goal.

(Performance in thinking is not just age-related: it is also affected by content, context, meaning and perception.)

The link among all my points is, I think, as one of my group suggested:

> the theme of development. Although we know a considerable amount about the stages of development, we are still remarkably ignorant about processes underlying development. This raises the whole question of the nature of maturation and the kind of interaction between maturation and experience or learning. All this seems very elementary, but . . .

We have had too much of the nature–nurture controversy, on whether heredity or environment is more influential. A more promising line of inquiry is to explore the interaction of the 'instructional' and the 'organismic'. Within the term 'instructional', I would include all the events, both planned and incidental, from which we learn, and clearly a strong element in future research must be concerned with the planned, deliberate part of this, namely, the curriculum, both content and method, in terms of its substance and structure. Strategies of learning are an important part of this too, and so also are studies of individual psychology, where psychometrics still has a part to play, both the testing of performance and the measurement of personality, attitudes and perceptions. The 'organismic' side is developmental psychology, and it includes concepts such as 'stages', which need to be constantly regarded with critical suspicion lest they become a disguised version of behaviouristic predestination: it also includes physiological studies, and cultural or sub-cultural influences. But the key part of it all is the interaction between the individual and the instruction, between the 'instructional' and 'organismic', for the interaction transforms both of the elements: the individual changes as a result of instruction (or, more generally, as a result of the experiences of all kinds from which he learns), and the content of his experience has meaning in terms of the structures which the individual imposes on it.

This is not limited to the early years of childhood, nor even to school-life, or to children. One of my replies summarises the whole argument neatly:

> Developmental psychology is increasingly thought of as life-span psychology. . . . All periods of development, at least to late adolescence, may be regarded as of equal importance, including of course the early years, but these should no longer be viewed as critical for later cognitive and social adjustment. The complex nature of biological and social processes in ongoing interaction is increasingly appreciated, and has, I believe, considerable implications for educationists.

That sounds rather like the end of the chapter, but I still have a few different points to add. I have concentrated on the promising aspects of the present state of educational psychology, but it would be misleading to leave you with the impression that the future is all rosy. There are two serious weaknesses which I would like to mention.

The first will be obvious to many, that I have had little to say about the *affective*, and have concentrated almost exclusively on the *cognitive*. Perhaps this is because of my own bias, which led me naturally to discuss this topic with people whom I know and who might therefore be considered a selected sample. I don't think this is the case, because several of my respondents made just this point, that at present there is a serious neglect of emotional and motivational aspects in educational psychology, and inadequate attention given to the social context, the importance of relationships and roles. I do not think it is correct to say that these aspects are wholly neglected nowadays. I think that they tend to be seen as belonging to other branches of psychology or of sociology, and so are neglected by educational psychologists.

That leads me to the second weakness in the present state, namely, the fragmentation of the field of educational psychology. As a result of this fragmentation, educational psychology has become too narrowly interpreted: it is defined by academic psychologists almost exclusively as learning or cognitive psychology, and in consequence it has lost much of its former 'territory' to other branches of the subject. It has surrendered curriculum studies, where Thorndike and others made substantial contributions to the psychology of the elementary school curriculum in the early decades of this century, and a new topic, curriculum development, has taken over, often without an adequate link with psychology. Social psychology and sociology have annexed large productive areas of ground; and even psychometrics has to accept the emergence of a new professional group (at least in USA), the evaluation experts, who now have their own journals and their own professional societies. Moreover, it is in danger of surrendering control to a specialist group of professionals. The Education Section of the British Psychological Society, which formerly was a very broad-based group of people, can no longer claim to be the academic body for educational psychology. Because of the policy of the BPS, the parent body, a large proportion of those who work in educational psychology, using a broad definition of that term, are excluded from membership, and have formed their own group, the British Educational Research Association. Because of membership requirements, the BPS is limited to those who have degrees in psychology, and, for education, to those who have post-graduate professional training for the schools psychological services. Consequently, there is a serious lack

97

today of a forum for discussion of the broader issues of educational psychology, a function which the BPS Education Section performed previously, but is no longer able to do.

Because of this fragmentation, educational psychology has lost its central position in education. Perhaps this is not wholly bad, for psychology held a dominant place for too long, but there is a real danger that psychology will be reduced to a limited ancillary role in education, and this is an error at the opposite extreme. In a recent book, *Psychopedagogy*,[27] Stones has suggested the revival of an old 'subject', the psychology of teaching, of the classroom and the curriculum, which he calls psychopedagogy, leaving educational psychology as a title for the clinical work of the professional people who staff child guidance clinics. The division is certainly a real one, but I hope that this split does not widen. Educational psychology is an integrative study, like education: it must draw on other branches of psychology and on other social sciences and its future development depends on this broad basis which I see as threatened by a narrow professionalism.

Notes

1 Standing Conference of Studies in Education, December 1969; *British Journal of Educational Studies*, 18, 1970, pp. 216-21.

2 S. Isaacs, *The Children We Teach*, University of London Press, 1932, p. 47.

3 E.g. P.E. Vernon, *The Measurement of Abilities*, University of London Press, 1940; G.H. Thomson, *The Factorial Analysis of Human Ability*, University of London Press, 1939.

4 *Times Educational Supplement*, review section, 26 April 1975; J.S. Bruner, *Beyond the Information Given*, London, Allen & Unwin, 1975.

5 J.S. Bruner, *The Process of Education*, Cambridge, Mass., Harvard University Press, 1960, p. 33.

6 M. Pines, *Revolution in Learning*, London, Allen Lane, 1969, p. 1.

7 P.B. Medawar, *The Future of Man*, London, Methuen, 1960, p. 102.

8 Op. cit., p. 103.

9 J. Downing, 'Psychology and the Bullock Report', paper read to British Psychological Society Education Section, 1975 (unpublished).

10 *Children and Their Primary Schools* (Plowden Report), HMSO, 1967.

11 *A Language for Life* (Bullock Report), HMSO, 1975.

12 Op. cit., p. 47.

13 Op. cit., p. 47.

14 Ibid., p. 48.

15 Ibid., p. 50.

16 M. Donaldson, *Children's Minds*, London, Fontana/Collins, 1978.

17 J.S. Bruner, *The Relevance of Education*, London, Allen & Unwin, 1972, Penguin edn, 1974.

18 Ibid., p. 18 (Penguin edn).

19 J.M. Anglin, Introduction to Bruner, *Beyond the Information Given*.

20 Conference proceedings: M. Friedman, J.P. Dase and N. O'Connor (eds), *Intelligence and Learning*, London, Plenum Press, 1980.

21 D. Broadbent, 'Cognitive psychology and education', *British Journal of Educational Psychology*, 45, 1975, pp. 162–76.

22 G. Pask, 'Styles and strategies of learning', *British Journal of Educational Psychology*, 46, 1976, pp. 128–48.

23 R.M. Gagne, *The Conditions of Learning* (second edn), New York, Holt Rinehart and Winston, 1970.

24 L. Hudson, *Frames of Mind*, London, Methuen, 1968.

25 F. Marton and R. Saljo, 'On quantitative differences in learning', *British Journal of Educational Psychology*, 46, 1976, pp. 4–11 and 115–27.

26 *British Journal of Educational Psychology*, 46, Parts 1 and 2, 1976.

27 E. Stones, *Psychopedagogy: Psychological Theory and the Practice of Teaching*, London, Methuen, 1979.

5 The sociology of education

Brian Davies

The central purpose of any brand of application of sociology is to 'look behind' the surface reasons for our social arrangements. This makes it a dangerous craft. Quite often the danger seems to be turned inward as sociologists of differing persuasions lacerate one another in paradigmatic battle. When they look out at schools or families or the state or whatever, they seem, even more often, to offer explanations of events in terms of some deified ideal, either of a methodological or theoretical kind. This is somewhat inevitable, of course, in any young and self-conscious discipline, where scepticism is liable to become either rather disorganised or tied to a dominant orthodoxy. It is made doubly so in sociology the objects of whose interests are numerous as human activities and include the processes of social change and stability themselves. This takes any version of sociology deep into the problems of power and legitimacy (questions about existing patterns of rights and obligations), which are at once both moral and disturbing issues, given that no society exists without hierarchy and that part of the *meaning* of social hierarchy is *invidious* ranking of social attributes. Sociology therefore exerts a powerful and disproportionate attraction on those who would change these arrangements, usually in egalitarian directions. Such change is easier theoretically 'said' than practically 'done' and sociology tends, at least in part, for this reason, to be guilty of more concept-spinning than evidence. In recent years it has become notorious in the eyes of some by claiming that knowledge itself is reducible to some aspect of the social or material world. This clearly outranks the accusation liable to be laid at the door of any social science of being simply 'jargon-laden'. Many merely liberal sociological practitioners, not least within education, are exhibiting the inclination to 'retire hurt', weary of being regarded, by turns, as *parvenu* or devil. However, the sum of their analyses of education, no more or less than those of their more radical bedfellows, seems to incline to the view that schooling changes little in social terms.

This 'strawperson' I have outlined may not, of course, square with the reader's experience, if any, of sociology applied to education. To date, it may not have been imagined that sociology (and hence its application to education) is more than just one 'subject'. Even worse, it may actually be held that there is a single form of explanation that satisfactorily 'covers' the social. If this is the case, then I would hope to persuade the reader to the contrary. I could not hope to succeed, however, as a liberal unwilling to break heads or minds, if there is a devotion either to certain sorts of beliefs which are conventionally counted as being within the sociological fold, e.g. Marxism of the variety of Althusser (1971), Sharp (1980), or extreme doubt in the reality of anything outside of individual consciousness such as in Blum (1971). Such beliefs as these can, for example, serve to remind us of the extent to which in our culture we equate science with rationality, simultaneously canonise individualism and property and believe in social magic formuli. But their central message is that we have closed the gap between 'is' and 'ought' in a single synthesis. I would, to the contrary, want to insist that the problem at the very centre of any sociology – that of the link between *identity* at the individual level and *structure* at the social level – requires us to persist with more than one form of explanatory life, in the present state of the art. We must resist the understandable tendency to choose social theories that have written into them our preferred happy endings, especially if we have to abolish all others in order to bring them off.

I make no apology for the seemingly roundabout way of introducing this review of the last twenty or so years in the sociology of education.[1] There is little point in trying to understand them except by beginning with a view of how sociology of education has related to sociology itself. In the main, it has been a rather poor quality 'taker' from its parent than whom it has grown even faster, not least for institutional reasons concerned with initial teacher training, discussed below. Its emphasis over thirty years appears to have changed from who has what access to the 'good thing' called education to what are the manifold effects of the dubious process which we call schooling. The underlying concern throughout has been with social inequality and education, inevitably in view of the besottedness of sociology at large with the same issues: narrow definitions of the issue in terms of which children of what class get into schools of different kinds have turned into a complex concern for questions of the determination and nature of processes that take place in family, classroom, school, work and other relevant sites. The opportunity early this century to define the sociology of education in such broad terms as these which were explicit in the works of Durkheim and Weber, and largely implicit in those of Marx, was killed by the narrowing effect of the main theoretical school which dominated sociology at large from the late 1930s on – the structural functionalism of Talcott Parsons. This inevitably became the main 'outlook' of socio-logy of education until the 1960s. Its emphasis lay on the functional and systemic interrelatedness of education and other social parts rather than questions of cause or conflict. As Bernstein (1972, p. 106) pointed out, in Britain even our awareness of continental thought came filtered largely through the American connection. Roughly, for long we imagined that education was undoubtedly for the best in a highly improvable world that would look much the same only better when we had finished with it. Now, many of us would be forced to depict schooling as generating a great deal of 'bad' as well as personal 'good' in creating the conditions for the maintenance of an exploitative *status quo.*

Accounting for the change

An account of these changes that might itself claim to be sociological could draw upon a number of sources. I want to suggest three:

1 We could look at the changing character of introductory texts and 'readers', the latter abounding in a shifting field. This enables us to get close to the subject's public representation and to feel how it is that it inducts its young. Here we would find a lot of variety. For example, many American textbooks look much the same throughout our period and this must have much to do with the remarkable insulation of North American higher educational parts. Britain's are much easier to reach, given their very much smaller scale and the effects of our practice of annual external examination. There is, therefore, very much more (but far from complete) homogeneity and a great deal more 'up-to-date'-ness about the content of our books and syllabuses (panic spreads as quickly as calm). We have differing sorts of textbooks. Firstly, there are those which focus on topics, drawing from a range of studies to provide descriptively satisfying picture-wholes, with long chapters on class and educability, medium ones on classrooms and short to vanishing ones on organisations and curriculum (e.g. Banks, 1976; Reid, 1978). Secondly, there are those with the same structure but with more systematic attempts to weave in theory and with fewer 'gaps' (e.g. Robinson, 1981a). Thirdly, there are more narrowly thematic (though still theoretically eclectic) works like Hurn (1978), with its very American 'equality' focus. Lastly, there are 'single' perspective texts or readers, not only

arguing 'for' a particular approach but 'against' most others (e.g. Sarup, 1978). To have been initiated into sociology of education in recent years is as likely to have been a mono-theoretic experience as anything else. As Bernstein suggests, one is more likely to have been socialised into an 'approach', with a character akin to 'a social movement or sect which immediately defines the nature of the subject by redefining what is to be admitted, and what is beyond the pale, so that with every new approach the subject almost starts from scratch' (1972, p. 105). The trends in teaching away from and toward such absolutisms, are conflicting. The contracting market situation imposes new conditions. In the war of the paradigms, more prisoners are being taken, more mingling may result.

2   We might look at the subject's own meta-story by reviewing reviews and journal trends, the former from Payne in 1929, through Floud and Halsey (1958) to Kloskowska and Martinotti (1977), the latter narrowly through *Educational Sociology/Sociology of Education* to the *British Journal of Sociology of Education*, as well as the major sociology and education publications. We would find plenty of evidence that the main focus between 1945–65 was educational opportunity and educability, viewed mainly along social class and, to a lesser extent, gender and ethnic dimensions. Fuller development of interest in 'the school' as an institution and curricular formations as socially organised knowledge comes later.

3   We might tackle head-on the institutional bases of sociology and sociology of education. Sociology has been pretty weak in the application of social analysis to itself. We have tended to prefer the high-flown comfort of concepts like 'paradigm' or 'problematic', 'epistemological community' or 'intellectual life' as 'practice' when talking about ourselves rather than analysing either our clan relations or material base(s). However, we have to face the fact that sociology in and out of education has swollen in particular contexts of

social and educational expansion. Then, just as now as it contracts, the 'times' must be expected to act selectively on who is recruited to what institutions and upon what knowledge areas preference will be bestowed. Let me immediately add that to say this is not to suggest that knowledge of intentions and institutions exhausts our insight into the truth status of our conceptual or research objects. But it is to say that we have spent far more time in other men's intellectual fields than in our own, pursuing the social basis of their knowledge. Good examples of recent work in our 'internal' sociology are found in cases like the investigation of the early interweaving of the objective and normative impulses of early American sociology of education in the *Journal* (see Szreter, 1980, for a recent summary). We know that in Britain and the USA, the best market for sociology of education has been in teacher training and education. Taylor (1969), Bernbaum (1977) and others have frequently shown that the relation represented a clammy and unrewarding embrace. Educational practice's historic floundering after effectiveness in classrooms, expected to deliver in turn both equality and efficiency, has created constant pressure to oversimplify its theoretical accounting. Not only sociology but psychology and other 'of education' disciplines have suffered, too. To put it crudely, but also I believe accurately, educational practice is about deliberately changing mainly young individuals and groups in directions which the changers believe to be for the better. We all know only too well that both personal and social changes are rendered a great deal more possible when we believe that they have a single, well understood cause. Alternatively, we shore up present conditions by showing that they 'have to be like that'. In sociology of education, as in other 'of education' disciplines, the constricting pressure upon theory, pressed into the service of practice, is reinforced by the urgency of the people-changing, society-making processes which constitute education. No society allows education to step outside of a narrowly defined range of policies and practices, oriented to the production of normal (approved, legitimate) forms of behaviour and consciousness in young people. Educational organisation, practice and discourse are soaked with many expressions and versions of good–bad in terms of 'behaviour', ability, motivation and so on. Any 'subject' invited in the flower of its youth to play handmaiden in the formation and change of such policies and practices in such a universal process (we know of no society that does it differently) was almost bound to experience a little revulsion in gaining an understanding of its own predicament.

Located mainly within 'training', sociology of education has not engaged the major attention of many of the best sociologists. Although it has drawn easy lip-service as to its importance, it may be that the instinct to avoid it has rested upon the long tacit knowledge – now highly explicit in many sociologies – that education 'takes' a society's imprint in relatively passive fashion. *Plus ça change, plus c'est la meme chose* – hardly a stirring call to intellectual challenge. Jencks is reported by Hodgson (1975) as saying of Harvard: 'When I was at the School of Education ten years ago, almost nobody who was literate was interested in education. The educational sociologists and psychologists, the educational economists, they were all pretty near the bottom of the heap. Suddenly, that's changed' (p. 35). But only to a limited degree. American sociology of education is still dominated by a relative handful of individuals who are mainly located in departments or faculties *other* than education. The position in Britain has been rather more complex, given the success of some few university schools or faculties of education (as well as other departments), and particularly their command of a central flow of publications, for example, the Open University and the Centre for Contemporary Cultural Studies at Birmingham. Mass consumption of their outputs has been generally uncritical.

Very great changes took place in the period between the accurate and deeply considered overviews of the field by

Floud and Halsey in 1958 and Ferge in 1977. Floud and Halsey argued that sociology of education had two focal points. The dominant one was the study of the role played by education in socialisation, in constituting the citizenry to play their part in the 'shambling sort of social integration' (p. 72) that marked plural, industrial society. In practice this was bound to spill over into the study of educational organisations and institutions, the other major focus, which was as yet neglected and required further development. This was to remain very much the case for another decade (and relatively so until the present day) during which 'equality of access' notions of educability (mainly concerned with entry to secondary schools, then higher education) were driven to the limit.

In British terms, certainly, the metaphors of 'pools of ability' and 'ladders of opportunity' were still those which provided the backdrop to the studies of class-value and aspiration differences, language patterns and so on. These were, in the main but not exclusively, imported from the United States (Tyler, 1976; Robinson, 1981b). The *Robbins Report* in 1963 on higher education, calling for much merited expansion, characterised the times much more than the Newsom Report of the same year which focused on the less able 'half' of the secondary school population and whose chief prescription was for more 'appropriate' curricular forms. These productions of the late Central Advisory Council characterise the managed partnership between British government planning and academic exercise which sustained a climate and context to which Turner (1961) gave the name 'sponsored' in terms of the mode of mobility through education that it exemplified. His idea that entry to selective (i.e. upward mobility oriented) education in Britain involved processes rather like that of joining a 'club', gripped the popular educational imagination and led to a spate of further typologising of educational systems in terms of their selective aspects (Davies, 1976, pp. 112–18). In over-drawn contrast, Turner had described the American system as 'contest', that is to say, it was regarded as more like an open-entry race from which individuals chose to drop themselves out. A slow accretion of information from empirical studies concerning the operation of schools and colleges over twenty years has been as nothing compared to the first shock delivered to confidence in these differing but beneficent systems by the Coleman Report (1966). This arrived somewhere around stage two of the three steps described by Ferge as portraying the road to disillusionment with reform trodden by education in parallel with other agencies attempting to ameliorate social inequality. Stage one had attempted to bring the child nearer to the school (with difficulty, for the differences rooted in social background often appeared ineluctable); the second attempted to bring the school near to the child and the third, with which it merged, countenanced the weakening or relativising of the social principles built into institutional structures by devices such as comprehensivisation or unstreaming or widening the definition of school leaving examination 'success'. In British terms, the latter was the period which spanned Circular 10/65, Charity James at Goldsmiths, the rise of the large comprehensive and the death of the form teacher, the birth of CSE, the beginnings of widespread unstreaming and contains that point where child and parental regard for educational forms tended toward the genuinely more conditional and even, in many cases, dismissive. School's authority system, inevitably in time-lag with social change outside, struggled to cope with the disaffection of the many 'ordinary' and 'less-able' children whose educational identities it sold short on account of its continuing inability to uncouple from its selective past. In US terms, Ferge missed the extent to which the school system had, on the contrary, since the institutionalisation of the grade system in the 1920s, found itself deeply marked by difficulties in facing children with high academic demands rather than problems of accommodating the ordinary. Indeed, the pressure of *Sputnik*, the perceived policy need to pursue 'standards' and excellence, had pressed the other way in shoring up belief both in the 'goodness' of schooling and in the efficacy of additional expenditures on selected innovation, particularly of the pre- and early school interventionist and secondary curriculum package types, in furthering liberal and technical functional hopes and purposes. In retrospect, this period has received a great deal of attention from neo-Marxist analysts who make it very clear that the intentions of any dominant group, whether liberal or otherwise, always have their class-defensive, conservative sides (Open University Course E353, *Society, Education and the State* is especially clear in this emphasis).

Coleman was certainly a major factor in generating what became the characteristic new pessimism of the late 1960s in which the geneticist explanation of IQ could revive and notions of class and ethnic apartheid rather than integration in education could begin to look attractive. If, as Philip Robinson (1981b) puts it, 'the moral commitment to reformist policies has been badly shaken', then it was here that the seed bed for denying 'liberalism' was laid. Roughly, its foundation was taken to be Coleman's finding that schools did 'not make a difference'. A little more precisely, he showed that schools tended not to throw up significant differences in the measurable attainment of individual children in terms of 'ordinary' expenditure variations. We were left with the rather dogged notion that the lower-class child was likely to gain from the presence in his/her classroom of upper-class peers but unlikely to benefit from the provision of a new playground or more books. Jencks *et al.* (1972), working for many more years on the Coleman and other data, added that equality of opportunity rested in large measure upon equality of condition. His injunction was to spend more on the 'less advantaged' but on account of criteria other than that of expecting increments in terms of post-school, superior life-chances. In effect he was saying that the poor simply deserve to have more spent upon them. In one sense, all the Coleman data was capable of telling us (and this had been the *played down* message in many another analysis of variance in pursuit of the bases of educational difference in terms of socio-economic measure) was that intra-group variations, as they were defined and in relation to the variable selected, were more impressive than inter-group differences. In Robinson's terms, the problem was one of providing an explanation that accommodates not only individual action but also social structure, that is to say which at one and the same time satisfactorily explains the frequently discrepant fates of individuals and groups, particularly in social class terms. Theses to the effect that 'school doesn't matter' had singularly little appeal either to communities at large or sociologists in particular. Vigorous assaults on the unwarranted use of class differences in family–cultural terms (particularly as perceived by and acted upon by school) to explain individual pupil performance were produced by analysts like Williamson and Byrne (1973) who wanted British school achievement data re-analysed in terms of all sorts of LEA expenditure variations. The 'class determinists' were almost bound to win, however, in the early 1970s, with neo-Marxism loosed, as Gouldner observed, as the new lingua franca of the young, new middle-class, professionalising sociologists, ready for moving up from their social constructionist games and who could point to the indications of their elders like Bernstein and Bourdieu that class control over the system's allocatory mechanisms was resilient as well as pervasive. We knew that the traditional 'old' upper and middle class of property and commerce had never lacked the means or resourcefulness to protect its interest. Now we were told that 'new' fractions of the middle class, those specialists in an increasingly complex division of work in our society in symbolic and cultural transmission and control (teachers themselves being a prime example), were equally adept at looking after their own. Lacking physical and financial capital they rigged access to intellectual capital via schooling as firmly as the capitalist-controlled non-educational production. The move to 'invisible', child-centred pedagogies in British primary schools (Bernstein, 1977) and the fate of secondary 'comprehensivisation' were both excellent cases of respectively general and local class subversion. In terms of the traditional question of equality of access to differing forms of secondary education, we know in retrospect, that the British system swung towards relatively more 'class unfairness' almost from the moment that it had succeeded in the early 1950s in getting something near to an 'ability–opportunity ratio' of unity (Floud, 1962). Then, a 'working class' accounting for 70 per cent of the population was getting about 55 per cent of the grammar school places in a context where given what appeared to be reasonable assumptions about the social distribution of the capacity to succeed at eleven-plus/'intelligence' tests (a misnomer, they were nearly always non-criterion-referenced *attainment* tests), its fair share would only have been 60 per cent. The promised land seemed awfully near. Halsey *et al.* (1980) have shown us, however, that lower working-class chances of access to selective schools were in retreat from the late 1950s. Accelerated by economic policy unwilling or unable to counteract the tendencies of technological change, the phenomenon of an 'underclass' in the midst of affluence has now emerged, a problem overlapping with but not identical to the fate of ethnic and *Gastarbeiter* (guestworker) minorities throughout Western capitalist societies.

Never has it been clearer than now in Britain that there is a naked face to the state's defence of the interests of capital which has direct consequences for the shape and resourcing of education. It is equally clear that the state's influence is felt more strongly via its operation upon the labour market, specifically at the moment, in generating unemployment and particularly youth unemployment. The freedom-through-knowledge bit about education is likely to be overshadowed for individuals by the bleakness of their concrete relation to specific labour market contexts (see Robinson, op. cit.; O'Keeffe, forthcoming).

If the class-educability, education-economy work had prepared us for a disenchantment with the capacity of the system to alter rather than merely mechanically distribute life-chances, then the work on schools, classrooms and curriculum up till the late 1960s was almost equally 'pessimistic'. The aspect of school organisation overwhelmingly researched was 'ability grouping'. Surveys tended to suggest little difference in terms of output variables, such as attainment, arising from group variations. Case studies, on the other hand, such as those by Cicourel and Kitsuse (1963) in the US and Hargreaves (1967) in Britain, suggested deliberate in-school processes of academic (and hence social, so it was assumed) selection based in varying degrees on class, ability, motivational and 'behavioural' criteria. Within classrooms, Parsons (1961) had suggested that an inevitable and largely class-determined assorting process took place in terms of cognitive and 'moral' (affective, attitudinal, 'behaviour') criteria. Henry and Jackson told us about the 'hidden curriculum' and suggested that it was potentially more important than the overt – a view which neo-Marxists like Bowles and Gintis (1976) were avidly to over-elaborate. The guilt of the educational tribe had already been established, albeit via false or at least unreplicable witness, by Rosenthal and Jacobson (1968) who insinuated that teachers manufactured brightness and dullness in children via the effect of their highly manipulable (and by association, fallible) views of them. A whole stream of increasingly sophisticated and complex research on such processes has failed to quite lift the stain off the individual teacher-bashed soul.

The same year, 1968, also saw the publication of Berger and Luckmann's *The Social Construction of Reality* which provided the solipsistic but powerful ink with which to print the new paradigms, already not only licensed, but also made mandatory for any Young Turk with ambitions for change, by Kuhn (1970). Both books were read with fearful shallowness, the former having its emphasis upon human capacities to 'make' knowledge and the latter its emphasis upon discontinuity and 'revolution' in disciplinary growth ripped quite out of context. Put into combination, they were held to advise sociologists and other persons of their capacity to 'dereify' that which predecessors had created. Structural functional sociology, with its *relative* emphasis on man-made-by rather than man-making structure was especially to be mown down, along with its quietistic cum symbolic interactionism which was merely agnostic as to whether the institution or the person was the chicken or the egg. The 'new directions' sociologists of Britain went straight for combinations of existentialism, anthropological doubt and post-Wittgensteinian 'analysis' with the single-mindedness of the philosophical *ingenue*. On the methodological side, positivism was castigated – Schutz, Garfinkel and Cicourel were invoked to join Kuhn as liberators from false objectives. Decades of honest grappling with problems of objectivity and bias in social science were set aside at a stroke of world-changing impercipience. The reverberations are still with us in the most absurd and indefensible parallel which continues to be drawn between sociological perspectives concerned with 'meaning' and non-positivism, as if we had discovered some new non-empirical basis for description of and generalisation about others.[2] In the late 1960s, however, such undeveloped delicacies mattered less than the academic-political events of 1968 which were cited as sufficient real-world grounds for 'rendering problematic' the official or established categories for educational dealing.

Young (1971) brought together difficult pieces by Bernstein and Bourdieu with Horton's anthropology, Blum's 'analysis' and the work of some ex-students like Keddie and Esland. Never neat at the time, we can see in retrospect that Young's editorial logic ran along the lines of accepting the validity of the arguments offered by Bernstein, Bourdieu and Ioan Davies, that is to say, that education was about the management of knowledge, a task which in total went beyond education itself. The possession of differentiated amounts and contents of knowledge was what the distributional processes within schooling led to. His logic broke with theirs at the point of not realising what type of difficulty was to be encountered in stepping beyond the limits set by such authors themselves in their differing views as to the 'nature' of knowledge itself – in Bernstein's case, a tacit form of knowledge base, in Bourdieu, the notion of 'structured structure', and in Davies, Gramsci's concept of hegemony. For Young, schooling was unequal (i.e. bad). It was not only difficult or inappropriate to remedy its defects by attention to children's 'home background', but almost certainly 'immoral' *pace* the Labov side of the debate with Bernstein: that is to say, black and working-class backgrounds were not only not deficient but 'fixing them up' constituted class dominance of a direct kind. Changing school organisation, teachers willing, was mere tinkering with form when it was content that required attention. The 'system' itself could be deconstructed by the dismantling of its knowledge content. Given the inconvenience of its total abolition, the alternative was to render it all 'the same' following Horton and Blum rather than Bourdieu, to argue that there was 'no difference' between 'common-sense' or 'everyday' knowledge and specialist knowledges. If all knowledge was held to be the same or equal, then it could not be used to differentiate its recipients or possessors. Inequality falls.

Alas, so does rationality, as Flew (1976) and others were pleased to point out, and solipsism reigns. In a world where any explanation (knowledge) is held to be as good as any other, not only do the trains not temporarily run but new integrating social and knowledge principles are bound to arise, and new hierarchies in both established. Bernstein's discussion of integrated codes proves curiously prophetic, very near to home. The simply deconstructing phase of 'new directions' which drew upon anthropology (e.g. Gladwin and Frake) for its vision of 'alternative logics' and early Marx and Merleau-Ponty for their humanistic 'engagement', gave way to the integrating principle of the *a priori* wisdom of neo-Marxists showing educational promise as to the fateful determinations of culture by structure, for example Althusser, Lukács and Gramsci. Keddie (1971) provided the empirical high watermark for the former, while Sharp and Green (1975) and Willis (1977) are well-regarded exemplars of the latter period. All appropriated interactionist fieldwork methods of extended observation and prolonged interview (with, in each case, very small numbers of subjects) to serve highly generalised and deterministic ends.

In America meanwhile, the social constructionist and Marxist strands developed rather differently. The ethnomethodology of a classroom researcher like Mehan (1979) has as much to do with going beyond symbolic interactionism into purified research techniques where the observer offers minimal intrusion or 'effect' as it has with wanting to change anything.[3] The ethnographic, case study approach to schools and classrooms in the US and in Britain with its emphasis upon careful description of and limited generalisation upon classroom processes, has continued steadily even if, as Delamont suggests, with poor levels of conceptual and theoretical cumulation (Delamont, 1981; Hammersley, 1980). The Marxist radical impulse is taken up in the US both by economists and historians. The archetype of the former, which belongs directly to the traditional concern with equality, is Bowles and Gintis (1976), with whom both O'Keeffe and Robinson deal fully. Re-analysing Jencks's data, they affirm that schooling is about the hidden curriculum as a route to the reproduction of the social relations of production. The assumption of 'correspondence' between features of the school and the work-place is tight, their delineations of mechanisms essentially psychological, that is to say, the experience of schooling generates the requisite habits and attitudes in the educand that are functional for his capitalist boss. In the mid-1970s, Gintis faced a British audience[4] unable to *recognise* a question which enquired as to the possible problems he raised for his own argument in asserting that it did not matter *what* was taught in school or anywhere else because all knowledge was arbitrary (i.e. equal, the same) and schools' achievement lay in *how* they put children through their behavioural hoops.

The Bowles and Gintis thesis was a curious jumble of 'soft' and 'hard' Marxist determinism. The American 'critical historians' who came to prominence from the 1960s on were mainly 'soft'. Katz (1971) depicts them as intrigued by how it might have been different, by the choice-points in human affairs. Wexler (1977) can talk of them and refer to the sociology of education as 'a small part of the larger struggle to gain control of our lives' (p. 27), presumably lives marked by the 'quiet desperation' alluded to by Thoreau, who he quotes with apparent pleasure. 'Our continuous lack of power is both expressed and perpetuated by reification – the projection of our human capacities on to external forces' (loc. cit.). We must 'reclaim' ourselves by reversing the process, render opaque social relations transparent 'through a continuous interplay of thought and action' (p. 28). This is mainstream early British 'new directions', several years after some protagonists of the latter had learnt that rendering things problematic involved rather more than simply taking thought in order to add cubits to one's stature, let alone altering objective states of affairs.

Present trends

We have come far enough along the road of a highly inexhaustive historical sketch to attempt to overview present trends in terms of substantive topic areas. Let me underline that this is *merely* a question of convenience – the work of many people in the field does not fall neatly within these spaces. Indeed, some explicitly attempt to correct, some to transcend them, including the recent Marxist vogue for arguing that incorporated ('sold-out'), fragmented and empiricist sociology of education must be abandoned altogether and education or schooling itself be viewed only as one site in the struggle for hegemony in which the socialist teacher should be careful not to isolate her/himself (e.g. Sharp, 1980). The socialist teacher in this sense, of course, is the Western Marxist. Ferge argues that the differences between socialist and capitalist formations and their educational systems as we know them are very little, on account of their past histories and current divisions of labour. Given the fact that neither are likely to arrange an educational–occupational lottery, she suggests that 'for the future manual worker, it is mainly the practical training in the factory that is relevant to his future job and life' (Ferge, 1977, p. 20). In the eyes of a Marxist like Sharp, Ferge's Hungarian realism is what gives Marxism a bad name. But one has to insist that a great deal of recent radical theorising has proceeded, as we have suggested, not only as if traditional canons in regard to empirical work did not matter, but as if all there was to be explained was a uniquely despotic late capitalism in crisis, whose social relations 'education can continue to produce, in a conveniently indictable form' ('Keeffe, 1981, p. 27).

Given that most sociologists do have substantive enthusiasm for 'topics' and that it is easier to name connections between categories, let me now proceed piecemeal. The divisions are purely for exposition.

(a) *Schooling in relation to the social formation, past and present*

The traditional mainstream concern with questions of opportunity and educability have now been swept along in the upsurge of structuralist and Marxist scholarship during the last fifteen years to make it *the* high status area of study within the field. In the USA, as mentioned above, the radical historians have worked both on local and national scale canvasses with varying degrees of quality, both in terms of historiography and conceptual excitement. At the one extreme,

117

Callahan's (1962) work is careful and seminal, Katz (1975) is rich in penetrating, conceptual jolts. At the other extreme, Spring (1972) is given to utopianism and iconoclasm, while Karier (1972) seems to me, taking no others, to become a prisoner of his own rhetoric. As a broad corpus, these and others have done much to ensure that the role of altruism in the historic rise of mass schooling is kept firmly in perspective. English counterparts like Wardle (1974) and Johnson (1981) are determined never to give it place. The historical dimension of a study like Grace's (1978) of the teachers of the urban working class is to be found typically wanting in its technical sense. A good deal of this thinness depends on an over-easy reliance on the written and official source – the smell and sounds of the classroom are very largely irrecoverable – as well as the overdetermination of key Marxist concepts in the area. It is as if we tried to reconstruct a recent history of the system with recourse only to Plowden, Boyson's semi-biographical panderings and the notion that truancy, indiscipline and gender differentials in subject achievement were all reducible to effects of the class struggle and patriarchy only. Richard Johnson (1981), from within a Marxist framework, argues for the avoidance of anachronism and for a more careful contexting of data when he suggests that the discussion of reproduction in terms of 'the language of conditions, requirements and needs, unless fully historicised, is likely to mislead' (p. 17). But again, I would argue, far too much of the delineation of the 'needs of different capitals' (loc. cit.) of which he talks is drawn from education *debates* of this century and the last. The dictum which he aims to realise is 'struggle produces structure, structure determines the possibilities of struggle'. 'Activity involves "struggle" because the social relations are asymmetrical' and 'structure is the product of past activity and struggle'. Structure determines struggle in the sense of there being 'limits to what even the most ingenious labourer can create from a block of wood and chisel, yet the outcome of her labour is not inscribed in the raw material and the tools. It depends also on her will and consciousness and way in which she strives to realise her aims in the product' (p. 18). Full historicisation of the rise of mass schooling, in this perspective, needs to have much to do with viewing it 'as an aspect of the transformation of the family in relation to capitalist development' (p. 20), paying full respect to the relations of the young for a 'place in the adult world' (loc. cit.), without assuming fit between certification and the labour market. This is an internally eclectic Marxism which dines out on the fact that groups do not change their place *via* education, while choosing to ignore its role in decentring the fate of individuals. It does, however, in my view, show an interesting development in the direction of placing at the centre of its programme the interaction of individuals/groups and structure. In this sense, although its focus here is politics and its categories are largely *a priori*, it has the form necessary to bear less than fully deterministic ideas about social and cultural transmission.

The main weakness of such Marxist historical approaches, which have taken to styling themselves 'political economic' in celebration of their belief in the interdependence of the two, is their over-reliance on global concepts with powerful internal theoretical warrants. Britain, in common with other Western industrial societies (social formations), has a liberal corporatist state, that is to say, behind the surface structure of a parliamentary democratic, egalitarian face it is increasingly dominated by and run in the interest of corporations which are increasingly multi-national in character. In the last hundred years in particular, work has become hugely deskilled (Braverman, 1974), the workforce across the job-structure increasingly proletarianised and social relations between capital and labour marked by changing forms of oppression and resistance. These concepts may be applied within the school itself, as for example by Apple, as we see below. Such approaches denigrate human capital theory, as in the case of Esland and Cathcart (1981) without an adequate representation of its nature, perhaps because they wish to avoid the implications of the extent to which our capitalist lives are

full of calculation, the extent to which we are deeply socialised into a market code. O'Keeffe, developing Bernstein,
argues that at the same time, in all advanced technological
societies, but most of all in the capitalist mode, it is the great
bulk of the educational system, itself a major site of production, which is furthest away from market principles. This is
not to deny its economic preparative function both in general
and specific senses. But it does suggest that the fate of its
least advantaged, least successful students *may* be related
to curricular concomitants of this insulation. In the context
of a capitalism unable to maintain post-war levels of full
employment, schooling will have the most dubious task of
motivating individuals for what can only be group 'failure'
through joblessness thrust upon it. The current rhetoric
of 'standards' and accountability is deeply related at a systemic level to this insulation of schooling from production,
which has both afforded the space for the growth of consumer (student) driven surplus of curricular output which the
market dislikes and the opportunity for this to be encashed
in employer and official rhetoric about the failure of school
to 'deliver the goods'. The relative autonomy of parts within
our school system has been real and the source of much good
as well as evil, the latter mainly reserved for the politically
silent, fully schooled but undereducated, during four decades
of 'expansion'.

O'Keeffe has drawn a good deal of his inspiration from
Bourdieu as well as Bernstein. He is not alone, however, in
disliking the 'tightness' with which Bourdieu has invested the
fit between schooling and social and cultural reproduction.
Bourdieu has given us concepts of great fertility – for example
'cultural capital' on the analogy of physical and financial
capital and 'habitus' to describe in fuller fashion the ideas of
home background and family types which have always fas-
cinated British empirical researchers. Bourdieu's concepts,
however, lack this empirical check upon their use and spin-up
into a web which outdoes that of even the most benighted of

British class determinists: only those escape into upward mobility via education who are touched in advance by the gift of appropriate family cultural resources (shades of Marburton, long ago);[5] their movement vents and sustains the system of domination, renewing talent at the top and depriving the bottom of it. Cultural and social change and stasis are completely interwoven, but there is very little specification of the mechanisms (as opposed to the sites) of transmission between groups and generations.

Bernstein continues to be the best known sociologist seriously interested in the same domain of questions and with a great deal more to say concerning transmission. He has returned, following his attempt to outline variations in the systemic relations of education and production (1977, ch. 8), to a fuller delineation of 'the process whereby what is regarded as a basic classification (class relations), is transmitted and acquired by codes which differentially, invidiously and oppositionally position subjects with respect to both discursive and physical resources', in conditions of advanced capitalism with its 'many different sites of unequal relations between social groups, gender, ethnicity, religion, region, each having its own particular context of reproduction' (1980, p. 37). Like Bourdieu, he is as we see, crucially interested in class in our sort of society and how class relations are passed on in the context of other related and different inequalities such as gender and ethnicity. Under the class umbrella, religious affiliation, gender, ethnic groupings and so on, all constitute categories of people whose outward relations are marked by power and who, within, are subject to varying forms of control. These relations generate and are governed by principles which, at the individual subject level, give people their position and potential access to the means to conceive of or produce change in their position. Communication within such a system is differentiated between 'dominating and dominated codes' which simultaneously remake and legitimate the class system which is not only shored up by 'belief' but by people's daily living-out of unequal relations. Hierarchical control over, and the right to judge the appropriateness of, communication is built into the system. These ideas are developed in relation to empirical work upon the classification principles of middle and lower working-class eight- to eleven-year-olds which suggested that middle-class children had greater access to a hierarchy of principles each with a different relation to the 'material base' than the lower working-class children. That is to say, the class occupational division controlled by dominant groups is accompanied by (creates/is created by) differences in children's perceptions of the range and complexity of the social and material world. Education is seen 'as a fundamental reproducing and producing agency crucial to (but not in close correspondence with) the class regulation of the mode of production, and crucial to the class regulation of modes of social control' (p. 10). School subjects/discourses have power which may be measured in terms of their separateness or 'delocation'. They are transmitted by teachers to pupils (who are both marked by membership of age, gender, ethnic etc. categories) as 'voices'. They justify their distinctiveness as natural and non-arbitrary despite the fact that they are related to wider social principles which change, while indeed 'a potential of the contradictions, changes and dilemmas generated by the classification principle itself' (p. 17) is the emergence of new voices. The production/reproduction of people (identity), categories (class, gender, etc.) and subjects (discourses) are co-determining processes with an internal dynamic of change and a rootedness in all of the 'outside' categories (the economic, the knowledge, the class), themselves subject to change, which they draw in.

Bernstein is here trying to extend his work on speech and knowledge codes to even wider sets of connections between people as subjects, class as our main social category and intellectual fields in Bourdieu's sense, while saying something about the *processes* involved which leaves space for the psychic and social creativity inherent in the operation of social structure and culture upon person and vice versa.

According to Atkinson (1981), in doing this he is making more apparent his affinity with European structuralism, whose recent common feature has been to link Marx with Saussure and Durkheim so as to show how the rootedness of our symbolic systems (language, subjects/discourses) in social life in general is more precisely understood when we add notions of power to ones of mere control. Bernstein, for all his delight in formalism and lapses into obscurity, attempts 'to provide empirical specification and historical location for the operation' of codes which 'not merely regulate language or curricula, but replicate social identities' (p. 92). Essentially, he seeks to retain the dialectic nature of person/society, in the context of class and other unequal relations. The fate of the individual is still a point of reference and interest.[6]

While it remains true that we need as much as ever to hang on to the fate of the individual in our explanations, disenchantment with individualist accounts of essentially collective phenomena has ensured the fall from grace of traditional, measurement oriented, analyses of educational opportunity and educability. One of Wexler's more perceptive observations relates to the extent to which, in the late 1960s, black groups came to realise that individualist models were inappropriate or even retrogressive in the analysis of the opportunity afforded to whole groups.

Marxist 'political economy' analyses involving moves 'outside an official ideology of education, which tends to view the school as a neutral, autonomous agent of social change' have, according to Arnot (1981, p. 98), attracted a great deal of attention from those concerned with women and gender and race in relation to education. Arnot argues that such a perspective has proven vital in relating

the structuring of the school and its products to the structuring of the labour processes and domestic life and can identify the forces and structures outside the school which could militate against any internal 'radical' reform.

> On the other hand, this political economy perspective has
> disadvantages in that it has not adequately described the
> *processes* whereby gender identities and relations are
> produced, reproduced and challenged within the day-to-
> day life of the schools. loc. cit.)

How needs to join *why* in the explanation. Accounts of the
processes whereby individual identities are forged in and out
of school need to interpenetrate accounts of structural kinds.

The shift in focus away from social class in global terms as
such – not because of change in belief in its importance but
rather because of the strength of acceptance of its universal-
ity – toward its manifestations in more precise forms, via
gender, ethnicity, religion, region and so on, strongly marks
present trends in analyses of access and distribution in
education. In analysing multi-cultural education, Mullard
(1981), like Arnot, argues that 'its history, its relationship
to the assimilation and integration approach and to the dominant mode of production form an integral part of its broader
social context' (p. 135). Its broader social context 'cannot be
unassociated from the interests of capital as articulated by its
various interest groups' (loc. cit.). However, he sees it as a
danger not confined to capitalist societies that

> ethnicity or the ethnic origins of black groups in society
> and black pupils in schools could . . . become, if unresisted,
> not only the basis for their oppression but also the way in
> which their experiential separation from and subordination
> to white groups is ritualised, controlled and secured.
> (p. 136)

One must agree both with his cross-cultural observation and
the necessity, within a society, of linking educational policies
and practices with wider social and economic contexts. In the
elaboration of the relations between gender and ethnicity and
education, we must not forget, too, that which we have
learned from our study of the 'working class', now moved
from the centre of the stage. The 'wounds' of pejored class,

gender and ethnic position are real but they do not destroy the autonomy or capacity for self-determination of their recipients. Murphy (1981) points us to the completeness of the false assumption which has overtaken the literature that 'the working class' fail in contexts where they invariably want to succeed. Musgrove (1979) points out what a seductive over-simplification and over-explainer the term 'the working class' is and experience of the whole range of social institutions tells us that 'separate' treatment almost invariably means unequal and less for dominated groups.

In an age which is more acutely aware than ever before of the ubiquity and resilience of inequality (whatever our view of its inevitability), there must be real space for a *politics* of schooling which encompasses both the insights of a Marxist analysis of power and belief in the fact that individuals and groups calculate rationally right across the social spectrum and take decisions on grounds of fairness and compassion as well as greed and envy. In a context where demands for social change are understandably more urgent on the part of the oppressed, where the nature of oppression is frequently mystified (as for example in our case of race) and where repression can be justified as inevitability, sociologists may actually bear both the good and bad news. At least we know that short of a realisation of a Western *gauchist* Utopia envisioned by the academic Left, who will choose wine in the morning, plot a little in the afternoon and dine about eight, hierarchy, like public transport, persists after the revolution. Private property may wither but occupations appear to go on forever. Class and class control merely change in form. The choices are within its limits. When Gouldner (1979), Bourdieu and Bernstein all converge on concepts such as cultural capital and 'new class' then we have an agenda around what Westoby (1981) refers to as the place 'of education in first, "techniques" of production, second, social relations of production and third, the formation and reproduction of a ruling minority' (p. 369). Our theorisation must reach from the state to states of mind.

125

(b) The organisational level of education

We are a long way still from having a systematic body of knowledge on the organisational properties of schools, colleges, local authority and central government agencies in education. This is very serious. They are all difficult to penetrate for empirical work except when the research design explicitly sets out to examine variations in child performances. I argue the situation 'is as if we had a sociology of "industrial" organisations confined only to elaborating how individual worker output varied with highly selected characteristics of some superiors' (Davies, 1981, p. 60). In this case, for workers read pupils and for superiors read teachers. Most of us, and especially teachers, are quite happy to rub along with a view of schools which holds that it is teacher personal characteristics that 'matter', given the child attributes delivered into his/her classroom. This incredibly limited piece of the conventional wisdom rests on a number of foundations. Negatively, it has a great deal to do with the fact that no one in education traditionally has had any great interest in looking behind institutional forms. What is likely to be thus revealed is not the neat unfolding of the happy plot foretold by the belief that education is good for you, but rather the child-differentiating drama dictated by occupational and class hierarchy, where the existence in school as in life of winners presupposes the reality of losers. All this is closely related to the way 'the work is done' (a characteristic feature of all organisations is that they 'do work'), that is to say, the broadly defined *technology* of educational establishments. It appears to me to be the overwhelming characteristic of educational organisations that they are marked by the weakest of the technologies that characterise people-changing institutions. There is flat contradiction between this and the 'improving' rhetoric surrounding educational processes. Values rush in to fill the absence not only of empirical information about teaching and learning processes but even the existence of a non-normative vocabulary to talk about them. If we test for this via teacher talk, we find ample grounds for our contention that they deal with pupils in terms of moral attributes rather than 'objective' characteristics. We very badly need work on schools which grasps the interplay between their organisation in terms of resources, decision-making features and so on, and school work in curricular and pedagogical terms. This must focus mainly on the classroom life of schools but it must not neglect the office, the department and so on. There has been much expansion (see below) of research in classrooms but a great deal of it has either dealt with them in unlocated 'one-off' ways or else has related their features directly to the class structure. It becomes increasingly clear, however, that the interaction produced in classrooms is crucially affected by decisions taken at the DES, LEA and school levels about grouping, curriculum, resources, teaching methods, time-tabling etc. It simply is not true that individual teachers take decisions on these issues for themselves and it is a question that has not been asked (it would be one of ferocious difficulty to pose) as to whether teacher or such organisational attributes are 'more important'. Researchers like Dahllof and Lundgren and writers like Westbury have broached some of the issues. Corbishley *et al.* (1981) is the latest of a series of reports on 'mixed ability' grouping which attempts to incorporate the organisational level of schools seriously into its analysis.

What still remains is the need for a wholescale attempt to apply organisational ideas developed in sociology mainly in industrial/commercial contexts to education, but without the traditional 'managerialist' bias of the area: the rational bureaucratic, human relations, decision making and communications, as well as the technological features of schools, require exposition. The studies of school organisation which we have to date, have largely come to us by 'accident' – as features of the pursuit of administrative questions, the effects of grouping, and the like. Much of the work is from the USA and carries with it the very important general message that schools must be understood in their local as well as societal context. Schools are, indeed, highly penetrated organisations in the 'non-capitalist state activities' sector which have peculiar difficulties in conducting their business rationally and present a crucial site for the development of either 'a genuine legitimacy of rule or an intolerable burden of repression' (Clegg and Dunkerley, 1980, p. 555). This is not overdramatic. Governments massively shape and fund schools and ration access by administrative rule in the non-fee paying sector. However, they leave effective determination of the running of individual establishments to a quietistic and defensive workforce. The consumer behaviour of parents and children is potentially more highly differentiated than the 'performances' of these establishments. In the absence of our capacity to formulate non-market principles of rationality in these areas, the situation is fraught with self-confirming unfairness. My own practical conviction is that those interested in change and improvement in teacher–pupil experiences within a given system had better not so much eschew the system and the classroom levels of change but affix their novelties to organisational forms which can be arranged and sustained.

(c) The study of the curriculum

Most of the recent work on knowledge and curricular forms has arisen out of speculation concerning the overall relations of schooling to the rest of the social structure. A good deal of the work has been based on ideas concerning ideology – roughly speaking how knowledge about states of affairs is used in the defence of interests, particularly ruling interests, and becomes embodied in relations between people – and hegemony. The latter is drawn from Gramsci and is concerned with the dominance of cultural forms by the ruling group in all societies. Both terms are frequently used with little precision and much rhetorical gusto. At worst ideology means merely bias or 'beliefs I don't like'.[7] Apple (1980) seeks ideology in the classrooms of schools which exist in capitalism in late crisis.[8] He is interested both in the *form* of educational practices (not just the 'hidden' in the sense of the values and manners that teachers emit but also the 'shape' of the content and its transmission) as well as the *content* of the curriculum. He inappropriately assigns the origin of interest in these categories within sociology of education to Marx rather than Durkheim. His analysis does not lead him to Sharp's conclusion that the study of education must be abandoned except as a subfacet of wider social struggle, but rather he wishes to embed it 'within certain long-term trends in the capital accumulation process' (p. 12) and changing work control. In particular, he sees what is happening in school curricular terms to be part of a wider tendency toward the commodification of social relations where even love and hope are available as goods and services. He concentrates more modestly on phenomena like 'pre-packaged sets of curricular materials' now widely found in schools. These increase technical control over (rather than by) the teacher and de-skill her while she is also being 're-skilled' in 'techniques for better controlling students' (p. 18). This process occurs because schools are lucrative markets. Students are produced thereby as 'possessive individuals', materials-paced, and oriented to the importance of technical competence. 'The work of a good pupil is the possession and accumulation of vast quantities of skills in the service of technical interests' (p. 23). Apple's hope is that we can find ways of 'resisting' these tendencies that are not self-defeating or do not compound the undesirable reduction of teacher freedom and control. He is borrowing from several neo-Marxist sources in this analysis; Habermas's ideas of knowledge and technical control, Braverman's deskilling thesis and Gramsci's idea of hegemony. The object of his work is thoroughly over-theorised and under-investigated. We have barely researched the surface of what is at work in the 'pre-packaged' curriculum and materials-paced classroom and are simply not warranted in making these assumptions. Reynolds and Sullivan (1980) are long wearied by the indulgent assaults of middle-class relativists on behalf of the 'working class' on school knowledge. Why will it mystify the proletariat while it appears to have done their mentors a deal of good? The correctly positioned Marxist must not fail 'to understand that the socially-shrewd bourgeois regard some forms of knowledge and thought as superior and therefore worth learning simply because they *are* cognitively and intellectually superior' (Reynolds and Sullivan, 1980, p. 191).

Much neo-Marxist sociology of knowledge, in its desire to demonstrate both the inevitability of change and its precise direction, neglects its real-world character. Magee describes Popper as arguing that 'change is the result of our attempts to solve our problems – and that our attempts to solve our problems involve, among other unpredictables, imagination, choice and luck' (1973) and that this handsome trinity require institutionalisation even though they are regarded as unpredictable. This is hardly likely to detain the spirit launched upon the praxiological form of life, where knowing how it is absolves one from the agony of pondering how it ought to be. Intellectual forms of life (however they may be demarcated) are not neutral *vis-à-vis* one another. Some forms are explicitly proselytising and resist requests to desist. Gellner (1974) argues that the rapid global diffusion of the scientific industrial form of life is the main event of our time and that doctrines in conflict with its superiority go to the wall. The exchange is merely for the possibility of a degree of material liberation. No doubt Gellner would distinguish between the sub-parts of our scientific form, more or less proselytising or change orientated. Magee thinks it a phenomenon 'whose utter extraordinariness is still . . . insufficiently pondered' that 'in under seventy years since his [Marx's] death a third of the entire human race . . . had adopted forms of society which called themselves by his name'. The connection is far from remote: there is no shyness about the praxiological form of life. Just as Habermas can claim that the culture of positivism (science is good and is good for you) generated by cognitive-technical interests (big business and its intellectual minions) suppresses the proper posing of reflective questions concerning its outlook (an empirical statement), so that it might be said that the Marxist dialectician absolved by the culture of praxis from the embarrassment of means–end disjunctures acts on. If you *do* know the end of the story then it seems only right that you should save others the bother of enacting the remainder. And there is certainly no need to check out existing states of affairs by research. A worthwhile sociology of the curriculum is still all before us.

(d) The study of the classroom

Many people looking at the above section will be offended by its implicit suggestion that non-Marxists had said nothing in recent years about the curriculum. I do not mean to say this, but I do think that it is the case that interactionist sociology of education has sheltered for comfort in the classroom. Ethnomethodology, it has already been suggested, was born out of an impulse to bring the descriptive reportage of interactionism down to the literally minute by minute account 'as it was'. It has from the start been very aware of its methodology, indeed some would say unable to transcend it. Superb accounts of verbal interchange and other symbolic emissions (glances, wriggles, etc.) remain exercises in social grammar building rather than speech unless they are linked to some wider account of their origins or purpose. Symbolic interactionism has also tended in the past to have to bear such a charge – pretty picture, but how did it come to be there? – but has become much more aware of its problems of showing relation between the everyday and face to face on the one

131

hand and the historic and large-scale (macro) on the other (see Hammersley, 1980). We have a remarkably rich and undercodified field which runs, in recent years, from Stubbs and Delamont (1976) to Woods (1980a, 1980b), which shows in Hammersley's terms that 'whereas in the past, descriptive adequacy was the priority among classroom ethnographers, in recent years there has been increasing pressure to link research in this area back to macro issues'. He sees this as difficult and even potentially dangerous:

> This pursuit of macro relevance must not be at the expense of ethnography's characteristic concern with grounding theory in fine-grained description of interactional processes and participant perspectives, nor should it result in us abandoning formal theory and, thus, forgetting how the internal organisation of settings mediates the impact of external forces, rendering the social world far more complex in structure than current macro theories would have us believe. (p. 67)

Amen to that.

Delamont is, as an equally committed ethnographer, highly critical of certain aspects of recent work, especially in the way in which 'each researcher stresses the uniqueness of her school and classroom, and neglects to read or use other research'. She is convinced that ethnography has breathed new life into the sociology of education and that 'recent fashion for talking about symbolic violence, cultural reproduction and ISAs [ideological state apparatuses] without providing any evidence about how educational institutions work, is no substitute' (p. 80). Her prescription for classroom studies is that Becker's warning that familiarity is the danger is still apt. She suggests that good work will proceed if we '(1) study unusual, bizarre, or "different" classrooms; (2) study schools in other cultures; (3) study non-educational settings; (4) make the familiar problematic by self-conscious strategies' (p. 74), either first-hand or through a proper familiarisation with the literature. It certainly seems to be better advice than turning quick dips into classrooms into orgies of criticisms concerning capitalism and its dupes. The difficulties *are* real. How *does* one relate the local to the wider framework? What are the translation rules? There is little wonder that the young researcher in the field feels that she is faced either with the overblown or the infinitesimally little in terms of the classroom work. It is people like Keddie (1971), Sharp and Green (1975) and Willis (1977) who have caught the imagination with great detriment to standards of quality in fieldwork. Each tells us that 'teachers' fail 'working-class children' in ways made inevitable by features of the wider society. Their jumps from their little bits of the here-and-now to their big story leaves some of their actors (usually teachers) pretty trampled.

There is a whole overlapping field between the sociological approach to classrooms and a much longer and more plentiful tradition of mainly 'systematic' (measurement-oriented) observation in the rest of educational studies (see McIntyre, 1980). The overwhelming orthodoxy in classroom studies (widely defined) has been the notion already mentioned in (b) above that individual teacher characteristics (especially his/her 'style') are most important in determining 'effectiveness', certainly as measured by incremental attainment in pupils. This type of context–process–product research has been rightly subject to a good deal of criticism, but in this area it has not hit the right target. Schlechty (1976) argues for a social theory of instruction in a thorough assault on 'teacherism'. The work of Dahllof and Lundgren points in the same direction. We must aim at the analysis of classroom process that descends to the specificities of their very varying social requirements. As already suggested, we should take 'how the work is done' with great seriousness and explore precisely how differing teacher strategies, pedagogical intention, creates modes of working which each have peculiar demands to make of pupils as to 'what it takes' to reveal ability in appropriate forms. In one sense one is merely reiterating that despite injunctions like Bernstein's as to changes in pedagogical forms, we continue to be seduced by, or stop our exploration at, the level of classroom oral culture. We must explore the structures beneath this level.

(e) Language in education

In practice my last category overlaps very largely with what we have been referring to above. It is not surprising given that the classroom is that special site of schooling's cultural (as well as social) transmissive task. In the last twenty years, we can distinguish between a sociolinguistic strand *per se*, long dominated by the work of Bernstein and reactions to it, commented on by Atkinson (op. cit., p. 88); a Marxist-influenced semiology which has for some grown out of it (e.g. Adlam *et al.*, 1978) but which, of course, stems more broadly from the application to language of the metaphor of base and superstructure to reveal that behind the apparently arbitrary relations there exists differential control over the 'means of enunciation'; an ethnomethodological and interactionist concern with speech; and a more 'ordinary language' concern with issues of 'register' and specialist vocabulary in school subjects. I refer above to Bernstein's development of his ideas in terms of his extended application of codes. On the application of semiotic analysis to the contents of written and verbal school texts, we must place some real hope that work of the same quality as that which we have seen in areas like the media and advertising analysis will soon emerge. Nothing can be more obviously the case than that the 'text', from the introductory reading scheme to the research monograph, has deep as well as surface structure, has form as well as content and that in education to date our approach to the importance of these issues has been shockingly neglectful.[9] Numerous classroom ethnographies have told us of teacher dominance of classroom speech (also well attested by the measurers), its convergent nature upon 'right' answers in question sequences and the tendency to equate 'learning' with the production of correct terminology, upon demand. Edwards (1980) in a survey of work on classroom language concludes that research since the 1970s has tended increasingly toward recording the actual words exchanged between teachers and pupils (rather than its mere enumeration in categories usually centring on teacher asking, controlling, approving, etc.), enabling detached analysis

> of the importance of stylistic divergences between teacher and pupils in maintaining or reducing social distance, of the typical ways in which language is used and interaction organized in classrooms, and of the narrow range of communicative options normally available to pupils. Such research has not so much provided large stocks of usable information as questioned the prematurely confident diagnoses of linguistic disadvantages and the communicative skills 'necessary' to educational success which were current before it. (p. 43)

He goes on to reject over-deterministic accounts without ignoring that 'there was always more to theories of verbal deprivation than an "obsession" with correct speech' (p. 35). Language work must go alongside interests in curriculum and pedagogy, as in Edwards's own case. The nature of the invitation to pupildom must be much more fully unpacked, stripped of its rhetorical and moral overtones and developed concretely in the context of specific modes of transmission.

Conclusion

My view is that we have passed decisively out of the age of innocence in education as in sociology. In the latter, those who refuse to entertain the notion that no single approach has sufficient warrant to attest society's complexity are interested in something other than sociology itself. The same is necessarily true of sociology applied to education. In sociology at large there is some real sign of a sinking of extreme differences and a convergence upon key ideas like Giddens's (1979) adaptation of 'structuration', which involves seeing the actions of individuals upon structure as well as the operations of structure upon individuals as embedded in, but not mirror-images of, one another. Much of the best analysis in education has and does work with metaphor or model of this type or is open to adaptation to such a model.

The educational identities of pupils are functions of experiences gained out of as well as in school. For a good deal of the first part of the last thirty years we asked necessary but, in retrospect, rather limited questions about which schools they were allowed access to, and we were strongly inclined to beliefs that individual and 'family' differences were so ingrained that little flowed in policy terms except the need to improve the selection mechanisms. Subsequent work on 'families' which has gone on to focus on categories such as gender and ethnicity, schools and their 'links' with economic, political, class and cultural domains shows us that this is but a tiny aspect of the issues. As Bernstein puts it:

> Intrinsic to contemporary schooling, irrespective of
> geography or ideology, are both the creation, management
> and legitimation of specialised differences and the creation,
> management and legitimation of various social inequalities.
> The question of the relation between, and the social
> assumptions of, the management of specialised differences
> and the management of specialised inequalities lies at the
> heart of a sociology of schooling.(1981)

More directly than in and around any other social institution, processes of power and control are focused in schools. There is played out the drama of who we want our children to be and what others will let them be, processes of making and becoming in which children are increasingly self-determining agents. There is no sociological approach to education that does not recognise the political and normative dimensions of these facts, none which would deny that if some social roles are demonstrably servile, dehumanising and 'anomic', our obligation is not to find good reasons for condemning some of our fellow men to their performance but rather, by technological innovation or a redefinition of our social and personal needs, to do away with such roles. (Entwistle, 1978, p. 184)

And there's the rub: the conviction that these changes can arise *within* education is shattered. Sociology of education must re-form around conceptions of change's nature and necessity which recognise that lip-service is the tongue in which all dominant groups have hitherto spoken in these matters.

Notes

1 This article is itself based upon my introduction 'The State of Schooling', *Educational Analysis*, vol. 3, no. 1, 1981, pp. 1-22, and I would refer those who would like further expansion of these themes to Hartnett (1981), ch. 2. There, in particular, I expand upon my rather cryptic assertion that sociology is most safely viewed in the present pass as more than one 'subject'. I am certainly convinced of this in the weak sense that the beginner is the more safely armed if she/he regards structural functionalist, neo-Marxist, interactionist, phenomenological, etc., approaches as different and competing, going on only most gingerly to establish their related and common objects. The price of avoiding this orientation is that paid by Fletcher (1980, 1981) who by dismissing many modern perspectives as mistaken outgrowths of historic insights leaves the substance of sociology to comparativist shell-collecting. He has his counterparts within other perspectives. In a more serious sense, I believe that we need to account for both the subjective and objective in social action/systems and that, contingently, theories of one tend to swallow rather than illumine the latter. I prefer to pay the price for the moment, therefore, of a seemingly irresolute 'perspectives' sociology because this allows me more scope in conceptualising the *play* between social structure and the person.

2 The truth is, of course, that the social sciences *do* have special difficulties of treating value-oriented action as datum and in facing the fact that all social knowledge touches interests. This has driven

people off the map in both directions, either into the poetic of 'we all know best but ultimately only ourselves', or 'materialist' explanations of the nature of interests which make knowledge their derivative.

3 *Learning Lessons* has a marked affinity with certain styles of discourse analysis and appears to be aiming at some 'grammar' of the classroom. Both its style and scope are remarkably limited. Read in conjunction with Mehan and Wood (1975) it illustrates for me why ethnomethodology, with its keen attention to the socially microscopic, has kept few friends in British sociology, despite the evident care and concern of many of its protagonists.

4 At a conference organised by the Open University at Balls Park College of Education.

5 *Marburton* was where Jackson and Marsden's 88 grammar school subjects went.

6 The most amazing exception to this in recent sociology of education is surely Althusser (1971) who inveighs against the 'subject' as blocking the route to a scientific (Marxist) understanding of reality and who reserves special opprobrium for the teacher whose task it is to extol to the child the virtue and necessity of individual effort and achievement. While it is easy to see the detrimental consequences of secrecy and competition, I have long doubted whether sociologists who have used his work approvingly realised that it actually abolished people as we know them.

7 Ideology has certainly become the sociological trouser-word to end them all. I simply do not have the space here to point out the difficulties and abuses which have abounded in its usage. I would suggest Larrain as the most reliable guide, invoke Roche's (1973) view that 'the sociology of knowledge cannot with integrity opt for some kind of reflex structural or economic determination' and suggest that the concept must be returned firmly to a Marxist framework where it picks out the decisive joint significance of economic determination and political practice. It has enough to offer in this region alone. We must recognise that terms like 'all knowledge may be put to someone's interest', 'ideology (breathing, friendship, sexuality?) is a lived reality' are fine so long as we are prepared to add that most useful of check-questions to them 'but is that all that it is?' They are all otherwise highly virulent cases of the genus 'when there is only one thing to say (know), it is a waste of time bothering with anything else.'

8 The terminology is taken from Finn *et al.* (1978), developed more adequately in 1981. The economics are unimpressive, though the social phenomena alluded to are of massive importance. The educational specifics, as opposed to the underlying reality, are wincingly

over-read. Tyndale, 'cuts', APU and post-Green Paper DES policy in equal parts mark out the massive increase in central government incursion into the life, including that of the curriculum, of schools. Sad though the fate of the unemployed teacher is, particularly as it has been produced by avoidable supply mismanagement at the DES (now approaching 2½ per cent of the total near half million stock?), what characterises the Machiavellian world of our masters more fully is their inefficiency – the DES 1981 *The School Curriculum* has nothing wrong with it that a seventy-period week could not cure – and the personal non-involvement via the withholding of their children from ordinary mass education which they insult us with. These failings are bad enough but they are as nothing in their implications for backlash in comparison to the discovery that it is the organisational autonomies built into the system that both allow for the buying of privilege *and* the withholding of entitlement.

9 The forthcoming work of Bill Cotton, carried out at the London Institute of Education, is a case in point.

Bibliography

Adlam, D. *et al.* (1978), 'A Matter of Language', *Ideology and Consciousness*, vol. 3, pp. 95–111.

Althusser, L. (1971), 'Ideology and Ideological State Apparatuses', in *Lenin and Philosophy and Other Essays*, London, New Left Books.

Apple, M. (1980), 'Curricular Form and the Logic of Technical Control', in Barton, L. *et al.* (eds) (1980), pp. 11-27.

Arnot, M. (1981), 'Culture and Political Economy: Dual Perspectives in the Sociology of Women's Education', *Educational Analysis*, vol. 3, no. 1, pp. 97–116.

Atkinson, P. (1981), 'Bernstein's Structuralism', *Educational Analysis*, vol. 3, no. 1, pp. 85–95.

Banks, O. (1976), *The Sociology of Education*, London, Batsford.

Barton, L. *et al.* (eds) (1980), *Schooling, Ideology and the Curriculum*, Lewes, Falmer Press.

Berger, P. and Luckmann, T. (1968), *The Social Construction of Reality*, Harmondsworth, Penguin.

Bernbaum, G. (1977), *Knowledge and Ideology in the Sociology of Knowledge*, London, Macmillan.

Bernstein, B. (1972), 'Sociology and the Sociology of Education: Some Aspects', in *Unit 17 in School and Society E282*, Milton Keynes, Open University Press, pp. 95–109.

139

Bernstein, B. (1977), *Class, Codes and Control*, vol. 3 (2nd edn), London, Routledge & Kegan Paul.

Bernstein, B. (1980), 'Codes, Modalities and the Process of Cultural Reproduction: A Model', *Pedagogical Bulletin 7*, Department of Education, Lund.

Bernstein, B. (1981), 'Preface', *Educational Analysis*, vol. 3, no. 1.

Blum, A. (1971), 'The Corpus of Knowledge as a Normative Order', in Young, M.F.D. (ed.), pp. 117-32.

Bourdieu, P. and Passeron, J. (1977), *Reproduction*, Beverly Hills, Sage.

Bowles, S. and Gintis, H. (1976), *Schooling in Capitalist America*, London, Routledge & Kegan Paul.

Braverman, H. (1974), *Labour and Monopoly Capitalism*, New York, Monthly Review Press.

Callahan, R.E. (1962), *Education and the Cult of Efficiency*, University of Chicago Press.

Cicourel, A.V. and Kitsuse, J. (1963), *The Educational Decision-Makers*, Indianapolis, Bobbs-Merrill.

Cicourel, A.V. (1964), *Method and Measurement in Sociology*, Chicago Free Press.

Clegg, S. and Dunkerley, D. (1980), *Organization, Class & Control*, London, Routledge & Kegan Paul.

Coleman, J.S. (1966), *Equality of Educational Opportunity*, Washington D.C., US Govt. Printing Office.

Corbishley, P., Evans, J., Kenrich, C. and Davies, B. (1981), 'Teacher Strategies and Pupil Identities in Mixed Ability Curricula: A Note on Concepts and Some Examples from Maths', in Barton, L. *et al.* (eds) (1981), *Schools, Teachers and Teaching*, Lewes, Falmer Press.

Dahllof, P. (1971), *Ability Grouping, Content Validity and Curriculum Process*, Columbia, Teachers College Press.

Dale, R., Esland, G., Fergusson, R. and MacDonald, M. (eds) (1981), *Schooling and the National Interest*, Lewes/Milton Keynes, Falmer Press/Open University.

Davies, B. (1976), *Social Control and Education*, London, Methuen.

Davies, B. (1981), 'Schools as Organizations and the Organization of Schooling', *Educational Analysis*, vol. 3, no. 1, pp. 47-68.

Davies, I. (1971), 'The Management of Knowledge', in Young, M.F.D. (ed.) (1971).

Delamont, S. (1981), 'All Too Familiar? A Decade of Classroom Research', *Educational Analysis*, vol. 3, no. 1, pp. 69-84.

Durkheim, E. (1956), *Education and Sociology*, New York, Free Press.

Edwards, A.D. (1980), 'Perspectives on Classroom Language', *Educational Analysis*, vol. 2, no. 2, pp. 31-46.

Entwistle, H. (1978), *Class, Culture and Education*, London, Methuen.
Esland, G. (1971), 'Teaching and Learning', in Young, M.F.D. (ed.) (1971), pp. 70–115.
Esland, G. and Cathcart, H. (1981), 'Education and the Corporate Economy', *Unit 2, Block 1, Part 1, Society, Education and the State E353*, Milton Keynes, Open University Press.
Ferge, S. (1977), 'School Systems and School Reforms', in Kloskowska, A. and Martinotti, G. (eds) (1977), pp. 11–25.
Finn, D. *et al* (1978), 'Social Democracy, Education and the Crisis', in University of Birmingham, Centre for Contemporary Cultural Studies, *On Ideology*, London, Hutchinson, pp. 144–95.
Finn, D. *et al.* (1981), 'Education and the Labour Market', *Unit 4, E353 Society, Education and the State*, Milton Keynes, Open University Press.
Fletcher, R. (1980), *Sociology, its Nature, Scope and Elements*, London, Batsford.
Fletcher, R. (1981), *The Study of Social Systems*, London, Batsford.
Flew, A. (1976), *Sociology, Equality and Education*, London, Macmillan.
Floud, J. and Halsey, A.H. (1958), 'The Sociology of Education. A Trend Report and Bibliography', *Current Sociology*, vol. 7, no. 3, pp. 165–235.
Floud, J.E. (1962), 'The Sociology of Education', in Welford, A.T. (ed.), *Society – Problems and Methods of Study*, London, Routledge & Kegan Paul.
Frake, C.O. (1964), 'How to Ask for a Drink among the Subanum', *American Anthropologist*, 66.
Garfinkel, H. (1967), *Studies in Ethnomethodology*, Englewood Cliffs, N.J., Prentice-Hall.
Gellner, E. (1974), *Thought and Change*, University of Chicago Press.
Giddens, A. (1976), *New Rules of Sociological Method*, London, Hutchinson.
Giddens, A. (1979), *Central Problems in Social Theory*, London, Macmillan.
Gintis, H. and Bowles, S. (1980), 'Contradiction and Reproduction in Educational Theory', in Barton, L. *et al.* (eds) (1980), pp. 51–66.
Gladwin, T. (1970), *East is a Big Bird*, Cambridge, Mass., Harvard University Press.
Gouldner, A. (1979), *The Future of Intellectuals and the Rise of the New Class*, London, Macmillan.
Grace, G. (1978), *Teachers, Ideology & Control*, London, Routledge & Kegan Paul.

141

Gramsci, A. (1971), *Selection from the Prison Notebooks*, London, Lawrence & Wishart.

Habermas, J. (1979), *Communication and the Evolution of Society*, London, Heinemann Educational Books.

Halsey, A.H. *et al.* (1980), *Origins and Destinations*, Oxford, Clarendon Press.

Hammersley, M. (1980), 'Classroom Ethnography', *Educational Analysis*, vol. 2, no. 2, pp. 47-54.

Hargreaves, D.H. (1967), *Social Relations in a Secondary School*, London, Routledge & Kegan Paul.

Hargreaves, D. (ed.) (1980), 'Classroom Studies', *Educational Analysis*, vol. 2, no. 2.

Hartnett, A. (ed.) (1981), *Educational Studies and the Social Sciences*, London, Heinemann Educational Books.

Henry, J. (1971), *Essays on Education*, Harmondsworth, Penguin.

Hodgson, G. (1975), 'Do Schools Make a Difference?', in Stub, H.R. (ed.) (1975), *The Sociology of Education: a sourcebook*. Homewood, Illinois, Dorsey Press, pp. 32-52.

Horton, J. (1971), 'African Traditional Thought and Western Science', in Young, M.F.D. (ed.) (1971), pp. 208-66.

Hurn, C. (1978), *The Limits and Possibilities of Schooling: an Introduction to the Sociology of Education*, Boston, Mass., Allyn & Bacon.

Jackson, B. and Marsden, D. (1962), *Education and the Working Class*, London, Routledge & Kegan Paul.

Jencks, C. *et al.* (1972), *Inequality*, New York, Basic Books.

Johnson, R. (1981), 'Education and Popular Politics', *Unit 1, Block 1, Part 1, Society, Education and the State E353*, Milton Keynes, Open University Press.

Karier, C.J. (1972), 'Testing for Order and Control in the Corporate State', *Educational Theory*, vol. 22, no. 2, pp. 158-80.

Katz, M.B. (1971), *Class, Bureaucracy and Schools*, New York, Praeger.

Keddie, N. (1971), 'Classroom Knowledge', in Young, M.F.D. (ed.) (1971).

Kloskowska, A. and Martinotti, G. (eds) (1977), *Education in a Changing Society*, Beverly Hills, Sage.

Kuhn, T.S. (1970), *The Structure of Scientific Revolutions*, University of Chicago Press.

Labov, W. (1972), 'The Logic of Non-Standard English', in Giglioli, P. (ed.) (1972), *Language and Social Context*, Harmondsworth, Penguin.

Larrain, J. (1979), *The Concept of Ideology*, London, Hutchinson.

Lukács, G. (1971), *History and Class Consciousness*, London, Merlin.

Lundgren, U.P. (1972), *Frame Factors and the Teaching Process*, Gleerup, Almquist.

Lundgren, U.P. (1977), *Model Analysis of Pedagogical Processes*, Gleerup, Almquist.

McIntyre, D.I. (1980), 'Systematic Observation of Classroom Activities, *Educational Analysis*, vol. 2, no. 2, pp. 3–30.

Magee, B. (1973), *Popper*, London, Fontana.

Mehan, H. (1979), *Learning Lessons*, Cambridge, Mass., Harvard University Press.

Mehan, H. and Wood, H. (1975), *The Reality of Ethnomethodology*, Chichester, Wiley.

Merleau-Ponty, M. (1900), *The Primacy of Perception*, Evanston, Illinois, Northwestern University Press.

Mullard, C. (1981), 'The Social Context and Meaning of Multicultural Education', *Educational Analysis*, vol. 3, no. 1, pp. 117–40.

Murphy, J. (1981), 'Disparity and Inequality in Education: The Crippling Legacy of Coleman', *British Journal of Sociology of Education*, vol. 2, no. 1, pp. 61–70.

Musgrove, F. (1979), *School and the Social Order*, Chichester, Wiley.

Newsom Report (1963), *Half our Future*, London, HMSO.

O'Keeffe, D. (1981), 'Market Capitalism and Nationalized Schooling. The Socio-Economy of Education in Liberal Society', *Educational Analysis*, vol. 3, no. 1, pp. 23–26.

O'Keeffe, D. (forthcoming), *The Sociology of Human Capital*, London, Routledge & Kegan Paul.

Parsons, T. (1937), *The Structure of Social Action*, New York, Free Press.

Parsons, T. (1961), 'The School Class as a Social System', *Harvard Educational Review*, 29 (Fall).

Payne, E.G. (1929), 'Editorial', *Journal of Education in Society*, vol. 2, no. 8.

Popper, K. (1972), *Objective Knowledge*, London, Oxford University Press.

Reid, I. (1978), *Sociological Perspectives on School and Education*, Shepton Mallet, Open Books.

Reynolds, D. and Sullivan, M. (1980), 'Towards a New Socialist Sociology of Education', in Barton, L. *et al.* (eds) (1980), pp. 169–95.

Robbins Report (1963), *Higher Education: A Report*, London, HMSO.

Robinson, P. (1981a), *Sociological Perspectives on Education*, London, Routledge & Kegan Paul, p. 39.

Robinson, P. (1981b), 'Whatever Happened to Educability?', *Educational Analysis*, vol. 3, no. 1, pp. 37–46.

Roche, M. (1973), *Phenomenology, Language and the Social Sciences*, London, Routledge & Kegan Paul.

Rosenthal, R. and Jacobson, L. (1968), *Pygmalion in the Classroom*, New York, Holt, Rinehart & Winston.

Sarup, M. (1978), *Marxism and Education*, London, Routledge & Kegan Paul.

Schutz, A. (1967), *The Phenomenology of the Social World*, Evanston, Illinois, Northwestern University Press.

Schlechty, P.C. (1976), *Teaching and Social Behaviour: Toward an Organizational Theory of Instruction*, Boston, Mass., Allyn & Bacon.

Sharp, R. and Green, A.G. (1975), *Education and Social Control*, London, Routledge & Kegan Paul.

Sharp, R. (1980), *Knowledge and Ideology*, London, Routledge & Kegan Paul.

Silverman, D. and Jones, J. (1976), *Organizational Work*, London, Collier-Macmillan.

Spring, J.H. (1972), *Education and the Rise of the Corporate State*, Boston, Mass., Beacon Press.

Stubbs, M. and Delamont, S. (1976), *Explorations in Classroom Observation*, Chichester, Wiley.

Szreter, R. (1980), 'Institutionalizing a New Specialism: Early Years of the Journal of Educational Sociology', *British Journal of Sociology of Education*, vol. 1, no. 2, pp. 173–82.

Taylor, W. (1969), *Society and the Education of Teachers*, London, Faber & Faber.

Turner, R.H. (1961), 'Modes of Social Ascent through Education', *American Sociological Review*, 25 (5).

Tyler, W. (1976), *The Sociology of Educational Inequality*, London, Methuen.

Vaughan, M. and Archer, M. (1971), *Social Conflict and Educational Change in England and France 1789–1848*, Cambridge University Press.

Waller, W. (1932), *The Sociology of Teaching*, Chichester, Wiley (1967).

Wardle, D. (1974), *The Rise of the Schooled Society*, London, Routledge & Kegan Paul.

Westoby, A. (1981), 'Education, Inequality and the Question of a Communist "New Class"', in Dale, R. *et al.* (eds) (1981), pp. 351–72.

Wexler, P. (1977), 'Ideology and Utopia in American Sociology of Education', in Kloskowska, A. and Martinotti, G. (eds) (1977), pp. 27–58.

Whitty, G. and Young, M. (eds) (1976), *Explorations in the Politics of School Knowledge*, Driffield, Nafferton.

Williamson, B. and Byrne, D. (1973), 'Research Theory and Policy in Education: Some Notes on a Self-sustaining System', *Part 2, Block 5,*

Education Economy and Politics E352, Milton Keynes, Open University Press.

Willis, P. (1977), *Learning to Labour*, Farnborough, Saxon House.

Woods, P. (ed.) (1980a), *Teacher Strategies*, London, Croom Helm.

Woods, P. (ed.) (1980b), *Pupil Strategies*, London, Croom Helm.

Young, M.F.D. (ed.) (1971), *Knowledge and Control*, London, Collier-Macmillan.